STEWARDSHIP PARABLES OF JESUS

STEWARDSHIP PARABLES OF JESUS

By
ROSWELL C. LONG, M.A., D.D.

ABINGDON PRESS
NEW YORK • NASHVILLE

X

SET UP, ELECTROTYPED, PRINTED, AND
BOUND AT NASHVILLE TENNESSEE
UNITED STATES OF AMERICA

TO
MY WIFE

GOOD STEWARD
OF
THE HOME

PREFACE

THE matchless teachings of Jesus in Parables are timeless. The six major Stewardship Parables, used herein, are especially applicable to the materialism of the present age.

The materialism with which this book deals is not that which has its origin in the mechanistic view of life and results in a stupefying determinism. With the new admission of mobility, and the use of qualitative as well as quantitative measurements, science has about eliminated the need of a book on that kind of materialism. What we are concerned with here is the materialism that originates in an overemphasis on the acquisitive instinct and flowers in covetousness. Such a materialism preaches prosperity as its gospel, makes business its king, gold its god, and enslaves its devotees under the de-spiritualizing and unchristian tyranny of *things*. Stewardship is the sure method of escape from such a tyranny, for it helps Christians, encumbered with the luggage of life, to find abundant happiness through contribution of life, and time, and abilities, and money, as a means to the propagation of the Story and Person revealed in the Gospel. We meet the menace of materialism in this rapidly changing world with the measureless might of Christ's unchanging offer of personal and social redemption.

The plan of the book is exceedingly simple. Each of

7

the six chapters presents a different phase of the theme under a common design, as follows: first, a statement of the principle by Jesus in one of his Stewardship parables; second, a brief exposition of the principle; and third, illustrations of the principle from historical and current sources, including books, the press, observation, and experience. Gratitude is herewith expressed to publishers and authors who have generously granted permission for use of quotations that appear herein. This permission has been sought in all cases where the origin of quoted material could be traced.

The book is launched in all humility, and with the earnest prayer that it may be used of the Lord to produce practicing stewards. R. C. L.

CONTENTS

9

I

STEWARDSHIP IN THE SOCIAL ORDER

THE GOOD SAMARITAN

Luke 10: 25-37

Now a jurist got up to tempt him. "Teacher," he said, "what am I to do to inherit life eternal?" He said to him, "What is written in the law? What do you read there?" He replied, "You must love the Lord your God with your whole heart, with your whole soul, with your whole strength, and with your whole mind. Also your neighbor as yourself." "A right answer!" said Jesus; "do that and you will live." Anxious to make an excuse for himself, however, he said to Jesus, "But who is my neighbor?" Jesus rejoined, "A man going down from Jerusalem to Jericho fell among robbers, who stripped and belabored him and then went off leaving him half-dead. Now it so chanced that a priest was going down the same road, but on seeing him he went past on the opposite side. So did a Levite who came to the spot; he looked at him but passed on the opposite side. However a Samaritan traveler came to where he was and felt pity when he saw him; he went to him, bound his wounds up, pouring oil and wine into them, mounted him on his own steed, took him to an inn, and attended to him. Next morning he took out a couple of shillings and gave them to the innkeeper, saying, 'Attend to him, and if you are put to any extra expense I will refund you on my way back.' Which of these three men, in your opinion, proved a neighbor to the man who fell among the robbers?" He said, "The man who took pity on him." Jesus said to him, "Then go and do the same."

(Moffatt's Translation.)

12

I

STEWARDSHIP IN THE SOCIAL ORDER

"When clouds appear, wise men put on their cloaks;
When great leaves fall, the winter is at hand;
When the sun sets, who doth not look for night?
Untimely storms make men expect a dearth."
　　　—*Shakespeare, "Richard III," II, iii, 30.*

THE Parable of the Good Samaritan, graphic, exact, and convincing, was set in motion by a jurist who "got up to tempt" the world's matchless Story-teller. It begins in answer to the question, "Who is my neighbor?" It ends in causing us to ask ourselves the question, "To whom am I a neighbor?" This parable expands our geographical frontiers and makes the words "neighborhood" and "neighborliness" consist not in contiguity of residence, but in opportunity; not in geographical location, but in answered human need, sacrifice, hospitality, humanity, and response to the needs of the underprivileged.

The robbers in the parable illustrate the type that says now, as then, "Life is for getting." "They stripped him," taking his property; they "wounded him," taking, as they doubtless thought, his life; and they "left" him, having no further interest in the human element, having secured their immediate financial objective. The Priest and Levite represent the present-day Church member who worships the "golden mean" of neutrality when hard decisions obtrude themselves in the social order and who, when the cry of the oppressed is heard in the land, greatly prefer that the pulpit stick to the "simple Gospel." The Priest and Levite type knows nothing of the Master's "give and it shall be given unto you" or of his "if any man compel thee to go a mile, go with him twain." And though strictly within the law, they neglected the injunction of Deuteronomy looking toward true neighborliness in the helping of a neighbor's ox or ass out of the ditch.

Neither of the first two types of this parable were acquainted first-hand with the principle of give and take. They were concerned about what they could get out of life; they were careful of their security and they were the grandchildren of the twin daughters of the horse-leach crying "Give, give."

THE FINE ART OF MAKING NEIGHBORS

When Jesus closed this story by turning to the jurist with the injunction, "Go and do the same," he meant that the Good Samaritan of the story was his idea of the way to make neighbors. For whenever the spirit of true stewardship finds itself in the presence of pressing need there is no need of the question, "Who is my neighbor?" In such an emergency the Samaritan gave of his time, talents, and courage, and physical strength, and money, and good will, and friendship until the need was supplied. He acted on principle, the Priest and Levite on law. The parable is a working illustration of happiness through contribution unprejudiced by creed or color, or caste or

14

continent. Notice that the real steward in this story did not allow his desire to help, or willingness to help, to be hindered by the letter of the law in the case, or by race prejudice, or by his own personal convenience, or the method by which the need should be relieved, or financial restraint. Some one has said that neighbors are made, not born. He whose ideal is success by contribution instead of by exclusiveness or hoarding of money or family tradition or culture and education, has the thrill of sharing with others. He is engaged in the fine art of making neighbors. His limit in the number of his neighbors is his desire to make them. He makes them out of half-dead Jews on the Jericho-roads of life; out of the noble but neglected people of the mountains; out of the masses of the colored race, or from the Indians, the aliens, or mixed races; he makes them out of the unemployed or the ill-employed; out of the "crooked sticks" and the social wrecks among the flotsam and jetsam of life. He contributes his neighborliness with no expectation of temporal return or reward for his service like the true Boy Scout with a daily good turn. His ideal is Jesus's "Inasmuch as ye do it unto one of the least of these my brethren, ye do it unto me." He knows that a happy life is composed of both give and take, and that one must first give if he would take happiness.

Dr. W. M. Taylor, in "The Parables of Our Saviour," tells the story of how his father was once on his way to the mill in rural Scotland with a heavy sack of grain on horseback when the sack of grain fell to the ground.

Dr. Taylor's father was facing the impossible task of getting the grain back on the horse alone when along came the lord of a near-by estate and, without seeming to condescend, gladly and quickly helped with his load. "How can I ever repay you?" asked the beneficiary of the lord's good turn. "Easy," he replied, "whenever you see another man as sorely needing assistance as you were just now, help him, and that will be thanking me." That is the true spirit of the Good Samaritan parable, and it needs practicing to-day. We have been the beneficiaries of the goodness and sacrifice of others and we have been helped hitherto. We must prove ourselves neighbor to a hostile world, rapidly becoming as hostile to our faith as it was to Jesus in the day he told this parable. The command is still, "Go" and "Do." George Bernard Shaw has said that a gentleman is one who tries to put back a little more than he takes out of life. It is a life of contribution to the needs of others that counts. Dr. G. A. Buttrick, in "The Parables of Jesus," shows that whereas this story began in a theological controversy it ends in a good description of first aid by the roadside. It was a case of personal interest in practical need. The Good Samaritan did not call up the Community Chest headquarters, or the Red Cross or Associated Charities. So far as we know he did not even report to the Travelers' Aid or the Rotary Club. He did the job himself and the greatest thing he gave to the wounded Jew was himself. Living to-day in this budgetized and mechanized age, when we exalt the impersonal in all of our machinelike precision of dealing with charity, we need to remember that we are missing much when we do not go along with the "wine" and "oil" and "shillings" given for aid to those wounded and lying by the roadside of life. Love radiates most when most in touch with real life and real need. Questions about eternal life may even to-day be answered in terms of room and board at the inn, as was the case in this parable. We have machines to dig, to plant, to plow, to cultivate, to reap, to haul, to manufacture, to sweep and dust, to sew, to carry messages, to write, to talk, to sing, to play, to vote, and even to lower us to our final resting places. But the "Good Samaritan" of the twentieth century is unwilling to lose sight of the contact of personalities that is the basis of real happiness.

The Church in an Acquisitive Social Order

Legitimate acquisition of property is a Christian duty. The Good Samaritan could share with others because he had something to share. If we retain the proper motive— namely, to keep the Kingdom of God first always—the acquiring of property is entirely worthy. If Christ is our partner in getting, our money success is laudable. We need more Christian men with more money, and more desire to share.

However, the most significant thing in the twentieth century is the reckless abandon of people of all classes in their development of the acquisitive instinct. The boiling of water in James Watt's kettle was the signal for the coming of the industrial age. It culminated in an industrial revolution in England in the latter part of the nineteenth century; it is responsible for the major social and moral maladjustments and evils of the United States to-day. What religion was to the Jew, what philosophy was to the Greek, what learning was to the Renaissance, industry and success in business are to the American to-day. Keen-visioned Churchmen see an accompanying drift in the Church toward externalism and secularization. In "The Spirit of Protestantism" Dr. Harris E. Kirk tells us that the modern church has been too content, too comfortable, too much at home and at ease in Zion; that she has forgotten her chief task of being a Good Samaritan to the unfortunate, the sick, the prisoner, and to the poor. The Church has builded better buildings, secured larger and better staffs of workers, made herself of better reputation in the business world, prided herself on programs executed, budgets raised, societies organized—all tending toward external conformity to big business and good business. Surely the Church has reached the point in her development when she needs to discontinue the major emphasis on "acquiring" equipment, standards, and programs, and begin more to emphasize her duty to "contribute" to the propagation of a Story and presentation of a Person.

The Church looks out upon a social order cursed by overdevelopment of the acquisitive instinct. More and more the money power is being concentrated into the hands of a few, until ex-ambassador James W. Gerard could say recently through the press that sixty-four men actually control America. After reading the list one Church periodical said editorially, "If these be our rulers, God help us." It is not in the concentration of wealth but in the impersonal element of the situation that our chief menace lies. Rarely does the real ruler of industry come in contact with the "cry of the laborer" in field or factory or forest. It does not help to say that the man at the top is as much a slave to his machine as is the man at the bottom. We must remember that while our President denounces, and rightly so, Socialism and Communism, in his King's Mountain and other speeches, we ourselves are guilty of, and responsible for, the great gulf between watered stock and big dividends on the one hand and dire poverty on the other. There can be little doubt of the fact that our economic life is ill-organized; that social maladjustments exist, and that the acquisitive instinct is responsible for building up the plutocracy of wealth, aristocracy of financial standing, and a "white-collared" hierarchy in this "land of the free and home of the brave"; this twentieth-century model of Democracy, where all men are declared as being "created free and equal." This is what brings socialism, communism, and other "isms." We are accustomed to decry these latter as "sins" and forget that "sins" of the economic order have produced them.

Undoubtedly the Church has come to a crisis, a testing time, a time when "wise men put on their cloaks" of spiritual preparation and protection against what bids to be a veritable storm. In the middle ages the Church attempted to put a curb on avarice and covetousness and over-emphasis is the acquisitive desire by banning interest-taking. Our task to-day is a cultural and educational task of curbing rapacity and ridding life's industrial high-ways of the "robbers" by beginning now with the young and keeping at the task until we have secured a change in the point of view of our citizenship. So long as we allow our young men and young women to grow up with the assumption that it is with the consent of the Church "that they should get who have the power and they should keep who can," and that the straight road to happiness is by way of getting all the money one can, so long will the Church continue to perpetuate a sinful, unsound, and superficial social order. There are clear evidences that there is a great spiritual hunger at the heart of restless multitudes both inside and outside the visible Church eager to hear the clarion call of the Church back to the road of the simple pilgrim who finds his greatest happi-ness in contributing to the needs of others out of a bounti-ful heart turned toward God.

Dean W. R. Inge, in "The Social Teachings of the Church," develops the theme that Christ came to preach a Gospel of spiritual redemption rather than social reform. He shows that from the heart comes all that defiles or exalts; that hard-heartedness, hypocrisy, and calculating worldliness were the sins that Christ gave most atten-tion to and that he condemned all overestimates of the importance of money. Since this is true, the Communist and the Socialist and the Laborite may also err as well as the big-business type of industrialist, for the love of money is not confined to those who have most. In the midst of social evils the task of the Church remains the same as always—that of building up of character rather than with external conditions; of cleansing the inside of the cup rather than the outside and of being the salt wherewith the social order may be spiritually salted. Partisan political alignment is a sure loss of leadership in the spiritual redemption of the individual, which is the chief task of the Church.

A Story from Marion

It was a dark day at Marion, North Carolina, in the foothills of the Blue Ridge, in 1929, at the height of the Mill Strike caused by a typical mal-order in the economic body politic. Five millmen lay dead as the result of the strike. It was the day appointed for the funeral and from the mills came men and women wearing overalls and calico. As the crowd from the hills began to gather that day there was tension in the atmosphere and the feeling that almost anything might happen. To the scene of the funeral came Cicero Queens, tall, gaunt, and grayheaded—a real product of the Carolina hills. There was nothing formal or ritualistic about the gathering. The hymn books were passed and a crowd of twenty young people who formed themselves into a choir led the singing of old-time hymns as the people gathered around the five plain pine boxes. There was some speaking and then a prayer from Cicero Queens that will never be forgotten.

Among other things he said: "O God, I have baptized a heap of people and I have been to a heap of funerals, but this is the saddest day that this old man ever saw. The Devil has got into the people. O God, what will become of the world if we don't get the Devil out of it? Help us to drive him away from here. Amen." "Amen," echoed the crowd all up and down the hillside. And "Amen" say God-fearing Christians everywhere to-day. Driving the Devil out of industry means driving the Devil out of the people in industry. It means that the Church will revolutionize the attitude, the thinking, and the conduct of men and women both high and low, both rich and poor, both employer and employed, so that we shall wish to "give" as well as "get" and contribute as well as acquire, and see that the chief end of man is to glorify God and enjoy him forever rather than to glorify the acquisitive instinct and pamper it forever.

The steward in industry knows how to drive the Devil out of the mill that he conducts, by just wages, Christian principles, fair dealing, square conduct, and human interest in his employees. The employee knows how to drive the Devil out by giving an honest day's work and loyalty in return for this same just wage of the employer. There is no field so great for the operation of the principles of Christian Stewardship and for constructive Christian leadership in the world to-day as the field of industry. Herbert A. Bosch in "Not Slothful in Business" calls attention to the need that we get the Gospel to work among the men and women in the workaday world.

He shows that the ever-widening circles of human life must feel the touch of Christ if they are to be saved or salvaged; that the home, education, culture, the arts and the sciences need the redemptive touch; that business and industry must look up and not around for inspiration to solve their problems. This is true of states and nations as well. The United Stewardship Council of Churches of Christ in the United States and Canada has recently issued the "Business Man's Stewardship Platform." This platform has had a most remarkable circulation among business men throughout the nation and is proving of great significance in giving the Christian point of view to the man in business. The platform recognizes three cardinal principles, which, if practiced in business and industry, will revolutionize the industrial order: (1) That every man's business is his best opportunity for service to God and his fellow men. (2) That every man is privileged to share with others what God has given to him. (3) That every man is obliged to account to God for all that God has given to him of business, home, education, and environment. We are depressed by a world-wide decline in gifts to missions. But how can we expect a man with money to support the sending of Christ to others when he has not taken Christ into partnership with him in his business? We are dealing here with the fundamental problem that the Church faces—how to put into the heart of the business man a new affection with expulsive power sufficient to drive out the acquisitive desire and make of him a Good Samaritan to others. The steward in business recognizes his work as a holy calling, a part of the divine economy and discipline of God's plan for world redemption. Through his business he seeks to render a spiritual service by operating and managing his business in complete accord with the principles of Jesus. The money that God intrusts to him he considers as equipment or tools, along with his talents and privileges and opportunities, by which he effects his stewardship. He therefore deals with his employees and business associates in the Spirit of Christ, "who came not to be ministered unto but to minister." Because he acquires and saves and spends and gives and accounts in partnership with Christ he is enabled to avoid covetousness, foolish luxury, unseemly pride, and excessive self-gratification. It is easy to get such a man to see the needs of the world because he has first faced his own soul needs. He acquires and saves and keeps his accounts in order to achieve life's real purpose and to live the abundant life. He sets aside a definite proportion of his income, usually beginning with at least one-tenth, as a "separated portion" out of which he may draw for Kingdom expansion. For this man, stewardship is a principle—it is "causal" rather than "casual." It points his life out of the morass and mire of sordid money-making and puts him and his business in line with the ongoing Kingdom purpose. Stewardship for him is not a legalistic whip to drive him into "paying his dues," but a principle to guide him into larger participation in the plan of God for the redemption of the world.

STEWARDSHIP IN THE SOCIAL ORDER

THREE KICKS IN EVERY DOLLAR

William Allen White, famous editor, recently with his wife willed to the city of Emporia, Kansas, a fifty-acre wooded plot along the river just outside the city, to be used as a park in memory of their daughter who died five years ago. In giving the park the donors stipulated that it should never bear their names and that they should have the privilege for the next five years, following the donation, of beautifying the park under the direction of the city's landscape director. The newspapers quoted Mr. White as saying, when he handed the deed to the mayor: "This is the last kick in a fistful of dollars I am getting rid of to-day. I have always tried to teach you that there are three kicks in every dollar, one when you make it—and my father's forbears were Yankees, and how I do love to make a dollar! The second kick is when you have it—and I have the Yankee lust for saving. The third kick comes when you give it away—and my mother was Irish, and that's why the big kick is in the last one."

This man recognizes that stewardship includes getting, saving, spending, giving, and accounting. If the thrill of trusteeship discharged comes to us, it must be after we have gotten a view of the larger stewardship which does not forbid or frown upon honest acquisition, right saving, or wise spending, but also includes generosity in meeting the needs of the world, before a proper account can be made to the Lord of the universe.

President Hoover said at Cleveland on October 2, 1930:

"I would again profess my undaunted faith in those mighty spiritual and intellectual forces of liberty, self-government, initiative, invention, and courage which have throughout our whole national life motivated our progress and driven us ever forward. These forces which express the true genius of our people are undiminished." What is this but a national recognition of reliance, for permanent progress in any phase of our national life, on the spirit of the Good Samaritan in the social order, upon the spirit of success and happiness through contribution rather than through ruthless acquisition that has its roots in avarice, pride, greed, and covetousness?

Dr. Thomas Cumming Hall lays much of the acquisitive desire for undue wealth at the door of the early settlers in America. He contends in "The Religious Background of American Culture" that John Smith led followers to Virginia more in the spirit of adventure and acquisition than to escape persecution; that the Massachusetts Bay Colony was a commercial and political undertaking with a small Puritan leadership; that the mass of the dissenting element came to America primarily to better themselves economically; and that in their analysis of American life, critics in both England and Germany have remarked upon the acquisitive character of our ideals and generally laid the praise or blame upon the shoulders of "Calvinistic Puritanism." Of course, with such a premise as this it is easy for Dr. Hall to draw the conclusion that by reason of its struggle for temporal power, rather neglecting its religious and racial traits, the dissenting element in our early American life laid the groundwork for industrial and capitalistic progress. His entire book, well documented by historical evidence, containing an excellent bibliography of reliable source-books, leaves us wondering where we got our information about America being built on religious faith. We turn to a book by Dr. Halford Luccock of Yale, "Jesus and the American Mind." The author has a reputation for veracity and painstaking accuracy. And yet he says that American history began with two words, "Land Ahead"! He pictures the Puritan in his last will and testament leaving the following things to the people of the twentieth century: a sense of God and responsibility to God, an inheritance of devotion to individual human rights, and a tradition of a sense of duty and serious application to the problems of life; but along with these, an exaltation of material prosperity, a religious sanctification of profit, a strong momentum toward the acquisitive instinct in direct apposition and opposition to the catechism definition, that "man's chief end is to glorify God and to enjoy him forever." Dr. Luccock does better than Dr. Hall by carrying his line of thought on down to the present. He imagines the Pioneer handing down as his legacy to this age—a wilderness subdued and conquered for modern civilization, a proving ground for new ideals, social strength, fortitude, and hopefulness on the one hand; and on the other, an aggressive individualism, a concentration on material things, a worship of the God of "getting on." Having made a geographical conquest, the pioneer leaves to us the problem of conquering the material forces that threaten to turn back the clock of spiritual progress. And then he has the Machine to tell of the legacy to the present age of a veritable fairyland of mechanical progress, a new release from drudgery, large comforts, heaped-up riches, and giant power-resources. Over against the good things, the Machine is pictured as also leaving to the present age the "ogres and demons" that people the fairyland of progress and prosperity, a spirit in bondage to things, moral handicaps difficult to overcome, poverty of spiritual power and purposes, and an age in which "prosperity" has developed into a morality and a religion. In the latter half of this picture Dr. Luccock has the support of such men as Stuart Chase and Harry F. Ward and Charles A. Ellwood.

THE PRESENT TYRANNY OF THINGS

It has been said that "things are in the saddle." We are told that the total number of "things" sold in the United States alone to-day is about 365,000 different articles. As compared to one hundred years ago, when the individual had seventy-two wants and sixteen needs, to-day the same individual has 484 wants and 94 needs. We are living in the midst of a civilization that glorifies prosperity with its whirling wheels, its multiplying "accessories" of life; and when a depression such as we had in 1929-30 comes, the most popular solution offered is that of selling more "things" to more people, of breaking down sales-resistance and building up a demand for more comforts and luxuries. What shall it profit a civilization to "acquire" the whole world if in developing this acquisitive desire we lose our own souls through a failure to "contribute" to the needs of the spiritual lives of ourselves and others?

The Church without a message to the individual rich or poor, harassed on every side by the insistence that material prosperity have the right of way in his life, is almost devoid of a message at all. For we are apparently on the threshold of the age of the "Bank Book," when property rights and profit-making, and "good business" and prosperity, are insisting that they have the right of way, leaving the traveler on the spiritual highway like the man in the parable, at the peril of the robbers, and often stripped of his spiritual heritage, wounded in soul and half-dead. To such an age as this the Church must bring the mighty impact of the teaching of Jesus of simple but powerful trust in an almighty God and freedom from the preoccupation with all the things that "the Gentiles seek." Pride, anger, envy, covetousness, gluttony, lust, and sloth were the seven deadly sins condemned by the Church of the middle ages. Of these, one, covetousness, stands out to-day as especially deserving the consistent and persistent condemnation of the Church. It is classed in the Bible along with sexual immorality and murder, but walks the streets of the cities to-day with head up, unrebuked because camouflaged under the general blanket of "prosperity." Edna St. Vincent Millay has well described the struggle of the soul in the present age, showing that it is possible to conquer in spite of "things":

"The world stands out on either side,
No wider than the heart is wide.
Above the world is stretched the sky,
No higher than the soul is high.

The heart can push the sea and land
Farther away on either hand.
The soul can split the sky in two
And let the face of God shine through.

But east and west will pinch the heart
That cannot keep them pushed apart,
And he whose soul is flat—the sky
Will cave in on him by and by."

The glory of the Christian religion is in its power of conquest over all the disquieting, oppressing, and clamoring elements in the secularized and externalized machine age of the present. Our papers and magazines are filled with stories of such conquest.

THE STORY OF AN HONEST DOLLAR

Captain Robert Dollar, at more than fourscore years, is such a story in himself—a story of the conquest of the acquisitive through contribution, a story of ships, seamanship, and stewardship. He entered the Oriental trade field as a young man. From the beginning he violated the accepted standard of how to do business in the Orient. He refused to enter a bar, take a drink, or do business in a saloon. To-day he sits in his office in the tenth floor of his own building in San Francisco, overlooking the bay where there is always one or more of his great ocean liners or cargo boats either resting in the harbor or handling cargoes representing every nation in the world. This Honest Dollar is one of the outstanding living exponents of the doctrine of Christian Stewardship. He believes that honesty is not only a good policy, but that it is a prerequisite for the Christian seeking safe conduct through the maze of things and contrary themes of the modern business life. With the help of God he carved his way to success by his heart, head, and hands. This clear-minded, square-dealing, thrifty Scotch-American, whose honesty was as native to him as his Scotch accent, refused to exploit the methods of his competitors and not only won the respect of the business world, but awakened the confidence of the Chinese as a missionary of the new spirit of stewardship in commerce. Although a Presbyterian, Captain Dollar's giving has extended to Baptist, Methodist, and other denominational fields, to the Y. M. C. A. and other great Kingdom enterprises. He is an illustration of the tireless aggressor wearing the Christian armor and fighting to success his commercial battles without compromise with, or yielding to, unchristian principles. He has been called the "Occident's great gift to the East; the most charming and romantic of living American capitalists and commercial magnates." He tells his own secret of success in the recent statement: "Unknown to a lot of people, I have been getting the help of the Lord right along." Seest thou a man diligent in the ideals of stewardship of business in such a mechanized age as this? "He shall stand before" the King of Kings unashamed.

Dr. Edwin Mims of Vanderbilt University has made a

great contribution to this modern Christian spirit of conquest over the material in his "Adventurous America," in which, among other things, he shows the mutual dependence of science and religion on each other; that whereas science abstracts certain qualities, and studies the man by sections in order to simplify the facts of observation, religion is concerned with the whole man, his purpose, values, and goals, as he relates himself to the supreme power of the universe in Jesus Christ who died on the Cross in Palestine. Admitting that this machine age tends to destroy individuality, Dr. Mims believes that the adventurous American with the right spiritual reliance will seek all the harder to make machinery a means rather than an end; avoid letting things take the saddle and ride mankind; and he will make Mammon the servant rather than the master. There can be little doubt that Dr. Mims is pointing us in the right direction. The Church can by illustration, example, sermon, and classroom teaching bring before the present and the rising generation the fundamental principles of Chrstian Stewardship and instill the dynamic ideal of happiness and success through contribution rather than by acquisition.

What the Man Told His Family

Let us suppose that a young people's society, seeking to dramatize the Parable of the Good Samaritan, shall assign to six young people the following characters in the story: the Traveler, the Robber, the Priest, the Levite, the Samaritan, and the Innkeeper. Those impersonating the characters in their imagination answer, each in his own words, the following question: "What did you tell your family when you got home?" The Traveler to Jericho says to his family in Jerusalem: "I am sorry to be late in getting back home from this trip, but when you hear my story you will not blame me but rather thank God that I got back alive. As I was going along what appeared a perfectly safe road, thinking about my sales-talk to the merchants of Jericho, a band of robbers suddenly burst in upon my reveries. Knowing that this part of the country was infested with bandits, I had taken the precaution, native to my race, of concealing most of my ready cash about my person and leaving only small change available in case they should rob me. This I readily turned over to them when they first approached. They evidently sensed the trick, for one of them immediately snatched away my outer garment, and, finding money therein, he with the others became so enraged that they beat me with their clubs until I became unconscious. Then it seems they stripped me of my clothing, and thinking me dead, dragged me to one side of the road and left me to my fate. When I awoke, whom do you suppose was pouring wine into my parched lips to revive me? None other than one of those cursed Samaritans. Cursed heretofore, but God be merciful to me if ever again I malign those people! This man rubbed oil into my wounds, brought me around, and then set me on his own mule and took me to the first inn. There he not only paid my room rent in advance, but left some money for the Innkeeper and told him he would settle any bill occasioned by my continued stay. But thanks to our God, I had to stay only two days. That is the story of why I am late, and also of why I am alive. Let us rejoice and praise God."

One of the Robbers: "We had a merry time with that Jewish traveling salesman to-day. We have been laying for him for weeks in order to catch him by surprise. One of our band had the tip that he was carrying more money than usual with him to-day, so we came upon him and took him completely by surprise, we thought. But when he so quickly turned over to us a small handful of pocket change we knew he was 'holding out on us,' so we stripped him and one of the fellows 'put him to sleep' while we finished the job right, getting a goodly sum of money. It's not my fault that fate is against me. I didn't ask to be brought into this world, and when the breaks are against us, as they have been lately, the only thing I see is to get our share of the other fellow's surplus. We have to live, I guess. And then too, my idea is that the world really owes us a living; so what's his is mine, and I took it. Of course we didn't mean to hurt the traveler, and wouldn't if he hadn't resisted us. I hope the government will fix it so none of my boys will have to rob."

Said the Priest: "I saw a sorry sight on the road down to-day. It seems that the robbers got that traveling man to-day. I have always told him not to carry too much money, and never to resist the brigands. He must have done both to-day, because they evidently took both money and life. I shall take this matter up with the officers of the Church. We need better provision for relief in such cases. I would have helped myself, but apparently the fellow was already dead, and I would have missed my appointment on the program of the meeting of the Priests at Jericho if I had stopped to look after the case myself. I referred to the evils of robbery and needs of relief, in my address to the priests. I think the Church ought to do more preaching along the line of honesty in business and government, and our relief societies should have more money with which to look after such cases. As my boys grow up I hope they will become great preachers of righteousness for such a time as this."

The Levite told a slightly different story. He said: "I am a little late to-night because I have just been to a meeting of the Council on my way home to report a case that should be investigated at once. The robbers 'got' one of our best men to-day, one of our best contributors and a fine fellow all around—the traveling man of whom you have heard me so often speak. His only fault was occasioned by his generosity, for he often carried too much money and the robbers got wind of it. They did a thorough job this time and he was barely breathing when I went over and looked at him. He has probably passed out of the picture by this time. There ought to be a law protecting a man on this road. Everybody knows that the territory from here to Jericho is infested with robbers, but nobody does anything about it. I would have helped this fellow myself, but I didn't have my first-aid kit with me, and only enough oil and wine for my own bare necessities. Then, too, there's nothing in the Levitical law which compels me to do anything in a case like this. There is something about helping an ox or an ass out of the ditch, but this fellow was too far gone. And a man can't be throwing his money around everywhere. I am trying to raise my children to be thrifty. What's mine is mine; I'll keep it."

The Samaritan came home unusually happy. "Hello, everybody," he said; "I am sorry to be late, but I have had a great time to-day. I have often had opportunities to help people of my own country, but to-day is the first real chance that has come my way to test out the idea of the Nazarene to return good for evil. Of course you know what the Jews and Samaritans think of each other. Well, on the road down to-day I came upon one of the most dastardly crimes I have ever witnessed. The robbers not only took the money of a Jewish traveler, but they came close to taking his life, so that when I got to him he was half dead and without clothing. So I used my knowledge of first aid to bring him back to life, put him on my beast, and took him to the hotel a little farther down the road. I have never seen a fellow so grateful in my life. I paid his hotel bill and told the manager to send me the bill if it was necessary for the fellow to stay over. If the Jew never repays me, what do I care? for it is only by such human kindness as this that we can ever bridge the gap of racial hatred. Then too, I try to practice what I preach to members of this family and to my friends, that we are stewards of our time, and abilities, and money, and whenever we have opportunities to contribute of these to others we must do it. What is mine is God's and others'—I will share it."

And late in the evening, when the guests had all retired, in the living quarters of the inn, the Innkeeper, or hotel manager, speaks to his family: "Well, this house by the side of the road has witnessed a real drama to-day. You remember that traveling man who always makes it here around noon? Instead of his putting in for lunch we had two dour-looking churchmen—a Priest and a Levite. They had little to do with each other, ate at separate tables, but both told the same story. It seems the robbers 'got' our good-natured and free-handed man to-day. The Priest was sure they left him dead, but the Levite offered some hope that life was yet in him. They both insisted that I send up for his body, and, if possible, bring him to life. I sent the porter out to get a couple of mules, and that was what I was preparing to do when you asked me this afternoon where I was going. But before I could get away I saw the strangest sight these old eyes have ever seen. You remember how the Jews hate the Samaritans? Well, what should I see but a Samaritan with the wounded Jewish traveler on his own mule coming up to the inn? And that is the fellow that you heard groaning over in the other room awhile ago. The Samaritan paid his bill and said he would take care of all expenses. Surely that is the spirit of this new Nazarene whose teaching is the talk of the town; and it will bring these people of different races together as nothing else. I am glad we have lived to see

37

this day when a man despised will go out of his way and, at great sacrifice of time and money, do a good turn to the despiser by sharing his goods with him. Surely we have lots to talk to God about in our prayers to-night."

And we might go on and on in our imaginations, picturing the effect of this story on the varying classes of people as from circle to circle and person to person it was repeated on that day and the days and weeks and years that followed, even as it has its dramatic effect when truly heard and acted upon in America to-day. Is it not true that these types are found in every community to-day —the robber, the neutral, the indifferent, the sharer, and the bystander? Is there sufficient moral stamina in the Church membership of to-day to insist that the principle of sharing with others shall dominate our social order? Is there sufficient respect for the human values, and power enough to resist the trend toward regimentation and standardization and uniformity?

Shall It Be Men or Machines?

Without attempting too much to moralize or spiritualize, but bringing this parable into the midst of our present social order, let us ask this question: Is it true that there are hundreds of thousands of the modern travelers on the industrial highway who have been robbed by the machine and machine-culture, and, wounded physically, morally and spiritually, left half-dead? Is it true that the Church should seek out and clean up the source of the robbers as well as act as a Good Samaritan to the wounded? It would be foolish and profitless in this place to attempt to bring a wholesale indictment against this age, for in so doing we not only indict ourselves who compose the people of the age, but we are also engaging in a game that has its teams on both sides. There is one man who stands out above others in his knowledge of, and spiritual interpretation of, the machine in our midst— Stuart Chase. In "Men and Machines" he weighs carefully the argument for and against the effect of the machine in our civilization—effects manifestly good, and effects manifestly evil. Among the good effects are such as increasing the life-span, higher standards of living, better coöperation among nations, decreasing of hours of labor, decreasing of cruelty, elimination of superstition and research into fundamentals of physics and chemistry. All of these are largely contributions to man's physical well-being. Over against the good effects we have: the menace of mechanized warfare, exploitation of men and resources, high-pressure salesmanship, the domination of the new ruling class whose god is the profit-motive, impersonality, progressive degeneration, overvaluation of industry to the detriment of agriculture, congested cities, noise, dust, smoke, and a high ratio of mental diseases. On this side of the scale we have largely moral and spiritual values. We are inclined to agree with Chase, that so far the machine has brought more misery than happiness. He shows that we have stepped up our power at least fifteenfold in the last century, and that whereas the total man and animal power of the North American and Western European continents does not exceed the equivalent of sixty million horsepower, the total horsepower capable of generation in the two continents is well over a billion! What a dare he flings to adventurous young America, to harness these billion horses, sprung from our brains, capable of death and destruction, running wild unless we tame them! Is Chase right when he insinuates that they came to us and remain with us to glorify the profit motive, and that human values, such as they are, must enter by the back door? All of us who have read it will not soon forget the merchant in "Middletown," who, speaking before one of the numerous clubs, said, "Our policy is to appeal first to style, second to price, and last to quality." Here is the definite sell-out to the machine age—the steam culture shifts from "goods" to "gold." If America is about to sell her soul for "acquisitive" gain, where stands the Church? We are reminded of the statement of one of Shakespeare's characters in "King John" who says:

> "Since kings break faith upon commodity,
> Gain, be my Lord for I will worship thee";

and later in the same play,

> "Bell, book, and candle shall not drive me back,
> Where gold and silver becks me to come on";

and then, near the close of the play:

> "This England never did, nor never shall
> Lie at the proud foot of a conqueror,
> But when it first did help to wound itself."

40

STEWARDSHIP IN THE SOCIAL ORDER

Every one who reads may find the story in Shakespeare's historical plays of what happens in a nation which wounds itself by the glorification of gain and suffers from "subsidence" of its foundations. We are greatly indebted to Galsworthy, undoubtedly one of the greatest character delineators since Shakespeare, for bringing this acquisitive instinct down to the present in his "The Forsyte Saga" in which he so skillfully portrays the Forsyte predisposition, by reason of heritage and teaching, to accept the formula that life's most important business is to have and to hold property; that man's chief end is to glorify property and keep it in the family forever. By mass production, regimentation, and standardization, the machine has put the premium on the "product" and made it possible for fewer men to control more and more of the output, and grow fatter and fatter in purse. It has of necessity crushed out the human element to a large extent, overlooked the development and the power of personality, and depressed the spiritual outlook. Now we are facing the question, "Shall it be men first, or machines?" One of the greatest men produced in America in the quarter century following the the close of the War Between the States was Henry W. Grady, the nation's great pacificator, and neighbor to all men everywhere. Shortly before his death he said: "No man can note the encroachment in this country of what may be called the Money Power on the rights of the individual without feeling that the time is approaching when the issue between plutocracy and the people will be forced to trial. . . . Our great wealth has brought us

profit and splendor. But the status itself is a menace. . . .
The abuse of this amazing power of consolidated wealth
is its bitterest result and its pressing danger." It is a
prophecy of four decades ago that is the problem of the
present.

But What Shall the Church Do?

It is surely not the function of the Church to reform,
but through Christ to redeem. The preaching of the
"simple Gospel" and the application of it by the Church as
a corporate body, or as individual members thereof, becomes the most complex thing we know anything about.
The principle of the redeemed life is trust in Jesus Christ
for salvation; the application of a redeemed life to the
social order, living in it, working in it, redeeming it, is
rich and varied. Let us notice some of the things the
Church may do to answer, in this time of amazing industrial development, the question of how we may put
men before machines.

1. The Church may teach her own members what is
indeed the chief end of man. She must somehow be able
to conquer the egotistical desire to pamper and pet the
acquisitive instinct by showing the ownership of God;
by showing that His is the power, and the wealth, and
the power to get wealth, that is given to the individual;
and His is the sunshine and the rain, and the component
elements that enter into the getting of wealth. It must
show the man that he owes to God a proportionate part of
all that he has as an acknowledgment of God's goodness

42

to him; and he must know the joy that comes from what Dr. M. E. Melvin calls "Royal Partnership" with God in making, saving, spending, giving, and accounting. Happy is the man whose Church has brought him to meet Christ in the market place and made Him his partner in industry. There begins life.

Dr. Harry F. Ward insists in "Our Economic Morality" that whereas Jesus set up the standard that a man's life does not consist in the abundance of things he possesses, the present industrial order denies it; that the method is competition, the motive is profit, and the end— possession of property; and that the theory of the divine right of kings has given way in modern times to the theory of the divine right of the money-makers. Which means that the Church must somehow get at the heart of the man; must somehow, by taking the long view of a social order built on redeemed individuals, seek to inculcate the principles of trusteeship in both the employed and the employer, and by the mutual interdependence of the Church, school, and government establish the righteousness of God in our midst.

2. The Church should preach and teach the value and function of the human personality. It is surely the duty of the Church in our present industrial order to protect to all the opportunity for health of body, mind, and spirit. If the ideals of the Christian religion are to be one with the ideals of politics, education, economics, and industry, they can find no better meeting ground than this—the physical and psychical development and protection of the

human personality. In "The Stewardship Life" Dr. J. E. Crawford devotes three chapters to the Stewardship of Personality, showing the duty and the means of self-development and self-investment. There is little doubt that under the amazing development of modern machine methods human beings have been more or less depersonalized. The tendency is toward the human robot, the mechanized, automatonlike man. The insistence on specialization and standardization has caused a drift toward a uniformity in thinking, a narrowing of intellectual interests, and a deadening of desire to explore new spiritual frontiers. The greatest "depression" is yet before us—a depression of spiritual desire and freedom of spiritual action by reason of external pressure of mechanical standards and outer conformity to prosperity requirements. The man of wealth is more in danger of being engulfed by deadly materialism than the man of small means. The Church may do much by sympathetic co-operation with such youth movements as the Boy Scouts and Girl Scouts, Four-H Clubs, Camp Fire Girls, and others seeking to inculcate the respect for, and development of, the functions of the human personality as related to head, hand, heart, and health. The rapid growth of these organizations is one of the most encouraging signs on the horizon. Of all the books that have recently come from the press that have the early beginnings of civilization in America as their theme, the most encouraging, perhaps, is "Puritan Principles and American Ideals" by Henry Hallam Saunderson. According to this author, the early struggles on the New England coast were a result of the eternal quest of man for a place and a freedom to develop his latent powers and for the possession of happiness through the proper coördination of the three institutions he most touches—the school, the church, and the state. He contends that American history is a story of the progress made in experimentation with the ideals that have to do with the development of the human personality. It is the duty and privilege of the Church to place the emphasis where Jesus placed it—the continual and unbounded development of the individual.

3. The Church needs to teach and preach with more zeal, and establish with more success, the law of love in the hearts of rich and poor, employed and employer, capital and labor. The writer lived for five years in the midst of an industrial community. Three of those five years were spent in one of the mill houses in one of the largest Southern cotton mills. There he came in contact with, and made friends with, people representing all the types in the Parable of the Good Samaritan. It is his testimony that vital Christian religion is the only sure cure of present industrial maladjustments; that human relationships depend for their success on right hearts; that character counts more than position, or wealth, or well-being, and that the only sure cure, and permanent cure, for "labor" troubles is the application of the principles of the Sermon on the Mount by both parties to labor contacts and contracts. It would be foolish as well as futile to excuse the Church for her lack of statesmanlike and Christian

approach to the industrial crises of the past and present. She doubtless has much to answer for by reason of her policy of palliation. But ruthless excoriation of the Church and of industrial magnates is equally futile. Without taking a seat astride the fence, surely there is an open door, a middle road which the Church-leader may travel. It is the road of the loving heart, the highway of the Golden Rule, leading to the open door of the individual heart, changing it and conquering the industrial disturbances in the conquering spirit of Christ. This does not mean that there is not a place for preaching on such passages as Amos 5 : 6-15, and other great challenges in the Bible to social justice. It does rather mean that blind and blanket condemnation of all capital, all wealth, all money-leadership, such as was often the case in the Gastonia, Elizabethton, and Marion disturbances recently, is of little avail unless such condemnation is a means to the end of putting the ethics of Jesus in industry by putting the fear of God in the hearts of the individuals concerned. Perhaps Ellwood has put his finger on what we are getting at here when he points out in his "Man's Social Destiny" that our great peril in civilization to-day is lack of balance, in that our spiritual culture lags so far behind our material development that we are about to lose control of the latter. What agency in the world can contribute to the restoration of this balance as can the Church? And how can the Church except she see the law of love in the hearts of the individual as the salt savoring the whole social order?

STEWARDSHIP IN THE SOCIAL ORDER

The Church as a Good Samaritan

4. The Church must be a Good Samaritan to the wounded, and the derelict, and the "casualties" on the industrial highway. The Church must not only help to build the fence at the top of the precipice, but bring the ambulance around to the place where those who have fallen, lie bruised and bleeding. True, we must help to clear out the robbers, improve the spiritual highways, and preach the duty of compassion, but we must also as Christians help those less fortunate than ourselves. The Church which is founded on Jesus, who gave us the Good Samaritan as our example, must contribute of her money to prove her neighborliness, and with no expectation of reward for her services! In the midst of an acquisitive society, and, a social order filled with "robbers," the Church alone is chartered as a steward who by her very character dedicates herself to the ideal of helping for the sole joy of helping. Use this measuring rod on your civic and fraternal and social clubs, all of which are more or less mutual in the give-and-you-will-get sense. The Church must increasingly make good neighbors by her constructive contribution of a determined stand for a square deal to the people by the roadside of industry and commerce; a stand against exploitation and paternalism while others fatten luxuriously at the expense of the exploited laborer. The Church will increasingly make good neighbors among the underprivileged classes and races. Speaking of the responsibility that we have to the Negro

race, Henry W. Grady once said: "Never has such a task been given to mortal stewardship. Never before in this republic has the white race divided on the rights of an alien race. The Red Man was cut down as a weed because he hindered the way of the American citizen. The Yellow man was shut out of this country because he is an alien and inferior. But the Black man, affecting but one section, is clothed with every privilege of government and pinned to the soil, and my people commanded to make good at any hazard and at any cost his full and equal heirship of American privilege and prosperity." To-day with the encroachment of the machine on the domain of the manual, the Negro is being forced to scatter, and has scattered far and wide over the nation. Great has been the progress of the race as a whole and brilliant has been the contribution of the race in outstanding individuals, but tragic is the situation and need among those left on the margins of the industrial communities and needing for their bodies and minds and souls the ministration of a Good Samaritan.

5. The Church must teach and preach the duty and privilege of Christian sharing. This applies not only to material possessions, but to the sharing of love and sympathy and vision and education and the privileges of Christian civilization. The press recently carried the story of the death of an eighty-year-old spinster, who died of natural causes in a $12-a-month Brooklyn tenement. She had lived there for more than ten years alone. Neighbors said she always spent money sparingly. When

the police took charge they found a purse containing $21.55; 340 bonds on the State of Virginia at $100 each; 21 mortgages on Brooklyn and Connecticut property, varying in amounts from $3,000 to $20,000 each; and nine bank books on Brooklyn and Manhattan banks representing various deposits. The entire estate was estimated to be worth half a million dollars, but it had barely kept the owner alive and she had shared with none! About the same time there appeared in the papers the story of Charles S. Bates, of Exeter, N. H., who nineteen years ago felt the call to send out native preachers, who otherwise would not be sent, to preach the Gospel where otherwise it would not be preached. His first thousand dollars went to Watts Pye, of Fenchow. He has gone on giving until he now has 262 evangelists on virgin soil in scores of centers in various parts of China, India, and Africa. His gifts have thus far amounted to an average of over $14,000 a year, for nineteen years. Thirty-seven thousand converts have been reported as a result. This man Bates manufactures shoes to pay expenses while sharing his vision of a Redeemer with others.

The Parable of the Last Judgment is a story in which man's entrance into the Kingdom of Heaven is conditioned by Christ on his willingness to share with his fellow men. Out of devotion to Christ have flown the streams of benevolence which have enriched the world by ennobled social relations and mutual respect.

Bishop F. J. McConnell brings us a helpful ideal in his "Human Needs and World Christianity" by showing that there must be three parties to a satisfactory business transaction if righteousness prevails—the two people who are doing the trading and the general public. He has in the background of his thinking of course the fourth party—God. He has put his finger on the great opportunity that lies before the Church, of showing that unless man is willing to share with the community, and with God, his stored-up knowledge, and ability, and money, there is little hope to gain the victory over externalism and secularism. Bishop McConnell agrees with Bishop Temple in urging that we keep uppermost these four things—the inviolability of personality, the fact of fellowship, the duty of service, and the power of sacrifice. That is exactly what the Good Samaritan did. And that is the Gospel of sharing with others and getting our personal blessings on the rebound. Stewardship is the attainment of inner happiness by contribution instead of outward success by wrong methods of acquisition.

II

ACCORDING TO CAPACITY

THE PARABLE OF THE TALENTS
Matthew 25: 14-30

FOR the case is that of a man going abroad, who summoned his servants and handed over his property to them; to one he gave twelve hundred pounds, to another five hundred, and to another two hundred and fifty; each got according to his capacity. Then the man went abroad. The servant who l ad got the twelve hundred pounds at once went and traded with them, making another twelve hundred. Similarly the servant who had got the five hundred pounds made another five hundred. But the servant who had got the two hundred and fifty pounds went off and dug a hole in the ground and hid his master's money. Now a long time afterwards the master of those servants came back and settled accounts with them. Then the servant who had got the twelve hundred pounds came forward, bringing twelve hundred more; he said, "You handed me twelve hundred pounds, sir; here I have gained another twelve hundred." His master said unto him, "Capital, you excellent and trusty servant! You have been trusty in charge of a small sum: I will put you in charge of a large sum. Come and share your master's feast." Then the servant with the five hundred pounds came forward. He said, "You handed me five hundred pounds, sir; here I have gained another five hundred." His master said to him, "Capital, you excellent and trusty servant! You have been trusty in charge of a small sum: I will put you in charge of a large sum. Come and share your master's feast." Then the servant who had got the two hundred and fifty pounds came forward. He said, "I knew you were a hard man, sir, reaping where you never sowed and gathering where you never winnowed. So I was afraid; I went and hid your two hundred and fifty pounds in the earth. There's your money." His master said to him in reply, "You rascal, you idle servant! You knew, did you, that I reap where I have never sowed and gather where I have never winnowed! Well then, you should have handed my money to the bankers and I would have got my capital with interest when I came back. Take therefore the two hundred and fifty pounds away from him, give it to the servant who had the twelve hundred.

For to every one who has shall more be given and richly given; But from him who has nothing, even what he has shall be taken.

Throw the good-for-nothing servant into the darkness outside; there men will wail and gnash their teeth." (Moffatt's Translation.)

52

ACCORDING TO CAPACITY

"What a piece of work is a man! How
Noble in reason! How infinite in faculty!
In form and moving, how express and
Admirable! In action how like an angel!
In apprehension how like a god!
The beauty of the world! The paragon of
Animals! And yet, to me, what is this
Quintessence of dust?"
            —*Shakespeare's "Hamlet," II, ii, 316.*

THE Parable of the Talents measures Christian growth,
not by equality of gifts, but by the individual fidelity with
which we develop our varying capacities. It is a wonderful and most convincing story about abilities and capacities
—their development or neglect. In the distribution of
gifts by the master who was about to leave on a trip
abroad, "each got according to his capacity." It is a story
about the development of the human personality and its
use in the Kingdom of God. That is the one thing that
Jesus was most interested in and is most interested in
to-day. It was to redeem the human personality that he
gave his life on the Cross. The interest of God the
Father, God the Son, God the Holy Spirit centers around
the crowning work of creation—man. When we study the
sciences and see the greatness of the universe we are
amazed at the greatness of God. The recent emphasis

on geography, geology, astronomy, physics, chemistry, and biology has been of vast benefit to all of us in expending our conception of the God of the universe. And we are constantly saying with the Psalmist: "When I consider thy heavens, the work of thy fingers, the moon and stars which thou hast ordained; what is man that thou art mindful of him? and the son of man, that thou visitest him? For thou hast made him a little lower than the angels, and crowned him with glory and honor." (Psalm 8: 3-5.) Speaking before a group of ministers recently an authority on bugs said, "The more I see of people, the better I like bugs." He is not in line with the chief interest of God, who, after forming the earth, the sky, the sea, and all that in them is, turned his chief attention upon the human personality, created in His own image. There God's interest has remained focused ever since.

Though beset by ominous perils through the impersonalizing process of the present machine age, and the rise of divers ideas and ideals that are battering away at the very foundations, the chief glory of the United States is the protection in her Constitution of the equal right of every citizen to worship according to the dictates of his conscience and to develop his abilities under the guarantee of life, liberty, and pursuit of happiness. It has been well noted by others that our government only guarantees that a man shall be free and unhampered in his "pursuit of happiness." Many outsiders may ask questions about our declaration that "All men are created free and equal" as if to declare a man free and equal will make him so! Of course to ask such questions is to miss the point of the greatness of America. Her guarantee is that each and every citizen shall have the equal opportunity before the bar of men and God to develop into that for which he is capable. Read the roll of our presidents, our leaders in business, war, church, and state, and notice the emergence from poverty and distress and lack of privilege to places of importance because this great Biblical principle is imbedded in our constitution and recognized in our social and civic and economic life. There is no gift too great, or position too high, to be bestowed by Church or state, that cannot be reached by the boy on the lowest rung of the ladder of conquest, provided he has the capacity to use the gift, or occupy the position, and the diligence to apply himself to the conquest.

> "You never can tell what the future may hold,
>   For the lads you carelessly meet,
> For many a congressman is doing the chores
>   And presidents play in the street."

The Parable of the Talents is illustrated over and over again almost before our eyes every day. The principle of growth by use, of atrophy by neglect, of commendation and condemnation applies to the abilities of body, mind, heart, and soul. Some day perhaps we will learn to fully appreciate what a keen analysis of human nature was Jesus.

THE REWARDS OF FIDELITY

One clear teaching of the Parable of the Talents, or

abilities, is that faithful stewardship in the use of capabilities is rewarded. First, there is the commendation of the master of the man who used well his ability to trade with the talents with which he was intrusted. He did not consider that they were his to do as he pleased with. They were a trust to him to be accounted for when his master should return. It surely must have been a fine feeling he had when he discovered that he could make money grow by wise trading. So that, even before his master came back, he had already reaped a rich reward in the commendation that was his within his own consciousness—the feeling of personal satisfaction. Just as the money grew by wise trading, so Jesus would have us know, our abilities and capabilities grow by wise use. Every one who reads this has doubtless had the experience of joy and satisfaction that comes from growth of a talent of some sort by reason of use and cultivation. There is an organization, rapidly growing, known as the 4-H Club which enrolls boys and girls on the farms in a great nation-wide emphasis on the head, hand, heart, and health protection and development. Perhaps the most amazing thing about our modern civilization is not its inventions after all, but the surprising capability and ingenuity of "the plain people" who grow and develop and astound the world by using God's endowment of native capacity to base their dreams of conquest on. Perhaps the world has yet to see what God can do with a man wholly yielded to Him.

In "All's Well That Ends Well," I, i, 202, Shakespeare

calls for the use of inner reserves in coöperation with the Divine, in accomplishing life's purpose and plan:

> "Our remedies oft in ourselves do lie,
> Which we ascribe to heaven: the fated sky
> Gives us free scope; only doth backward pull
> Our slow designs when we ourselves are dull."

The second reward of fidelity, in life, as in the parable, is enlargement of opportunity. The fellow who was given an additional and larger sum, after he had doubled his previous supply of pounds, entered into an enlarged field of opportunity. Just around the corner for every Christian there are wonderful opportunities for service, for soul-winning, and for investment of life. But God can only pour into our lives as our capacities will permit. Yonder beckons another rung in the ladder of Christian success and happiness and opportunity and privilege. But to reach it, to stand on it, and to survey the world from it, I must first be faithful on the lower levels of life. If I shut Christ out of the lower levels, I surely cannot expect to find him in the higher levels.

The third reward of fidelity is enlarged capacity. When we read the twenty-third Psalm and come to the place where it says "my cup runneth over," unless we stop to think, we naturally picture a big cup, a big blessing, a big banquet. It is well to remember that a small cup may run over as well as a big one, and that it is only when the cup overflows that others get a blessing from our lives. So long as we fail to go into the markets of life and trade there with head, hand, heart, or health, we are sure to fail to grow. But when we do present to our Lord each day an accounting of our abilities that shows an increase, we may be sure likewise of his invitation to enter larger fields of usefulness because we have larger capacities.

The fourth reward is the sharing of the Lord's fellowship in service. This is the reward of faithful stewardship, that we are taken into the partnership that has as its object the winning of the world for Christ. To the two who were faithful the master in the story said, "Come and share your master's feast." There is the real overflowing cup, that, through fidelity in the use of what we have, we may get the reward of being taken in as coworkers with God. Down the highway of life, together with the Master we go; over the rough places he will help us; when the going is hard he will encourage us; and when the burden is heavy he will help to lift it, "For my yoke is easy, and my burden is light," saith the Master. The requirement is that we shall, having received gifts differing according to our capacity, trade with them, cultivate them, encourage them, and thus increase them. "As every man hath received the gift, even so minister the same one to another, as good stewards of the manifold grace of God." (1 Pet. 4: 10.) As Paul said to his son-in-the-faith, Timothy, we must "stir up the gift" that is within us, if we would reap the rewards of fidelity.

A thought-provoking book is "The Problem of God," by Edgar Sheffield Brightman of Boston University. He shows us how science has expanded the mental horizon of people so that their appreciation of, and conception of, God has grown beyond measure in recent years. In like manner the author deals with religion, expanding from the tribal conception to the national and universal in its conception of God, while all the time the philosopher takes the current notion of God as his basic explanation of things. Another helpful book in this respect is "The Procession of the Gods," by Gaius Glenn Atkins. Nowhere in so small compass can we find the gods of ancient and modern people passing in review before us as in this delightfully written, daringly conceived, and scholarly executed masterpiece. And the big thing that stands out is the expanding conception of the greatness, the goodness, the forgivenness, the sacrifice and triumph of a life of trust in the Christian's God—the only true God. We are living in a time that demands great expansion of mind, body, and soul or we must suffer the excruciating agony of being crushed to death in intellect and spirit. Both of these books are excellent commentaries, without intending to be so, on the Parable of the Talents. No one would without hesitation take these books unreservedly to his bosom and indorse every position that the authors take, or the sentiments they express. But we need the mental and spiritual stimulation that they give in order to be found faithful in the development of the gifts that God has bestowed upon us.

There are matchless rewards to the young man or young woman, the mature man or woman who has discovered that, though the physical body may have reached its full growth, physical and mental and spiritual opportunities cannot be fully utilized and occupied unless there is continual expansion. Expansion comes through wise trading with the forces of the body, mind, and soul. The markets of life are always open for the man who knows how or is willing to learn how to trade wisely therein. The rewards are always waiting on ahead, in the pathway of real life, to the one who, trusted of the Father with gifts, differing according to capacity, has been found faithful and renders a daily account which indicates growth by use. "Capital, you excellent and trusty servant. You have been trusty in charge of a small sum. I will put you in charge of a large sum."

From "Goose Girl" to World Figure

Jan Christian Smuts began his stewardship as a "goose girl." As there were no girls in the family in which he was raised in South Africa, he was assigned to this menial task as his first job as a boy. For four years "Jannie," as he was known, held this job. Because he was faithful and uncomplaining he was made overseer of the pigs, and later of the sheep, and later still of the cows. It is a significant fact that the word "steward" comes from the old English words "stig" and "weard," meaning "ward of the pigs" or keeper of the pigsty. So, this man was beginning his stewardship at the place it got its name. The ambition of the lad was to be in charge of the horses. He was raised near Riebeek, in the great grain and cattle section of South Africa, and his father's farm stretched from the base of Malmsbury Mountains to the Atlantic Ocean. The great ambition was realized at twelve years of age when his father made him steward of the horses. He did not mind rising at four in the morning when there came with the day always the thrill of fulfilling his desire. For two years before he went away to school he continued in this task, his faithfulness and trustworthiness being a prediction of what was to come in later life.

We may disagree with some of the ideas of this great man, but we are bound to see him the enthroned ruler of thousands of hearts, though he wears no temporal crown, nor carries the insignia of a conqueror. He is an apostle of peace, world statesman, Christian leader, and friend of the masses; friend of the Boer, friend of the oppressed, and friend of Christ. He delights in marshaling the people of the world, not with the baton of the soldier, but with the sign of the Cross and the banner of peace. Eagerly sought in all parts of the world because of his giant intellect and high vision of world need, he remains the humble servant of God. He believes that the strong nations are God-ordained stewards of weak nations and peoples. When asked on a recent trip to the United States to give his opinion of Christian missions, he answered without hesitation: "Christian missions provide the only agency I know that is powerful enough to enable both black and white folks . . . to realize their respective destinies and yet live together in peace." Which is another way of saying that our stewardship of the Gospel of Christ, if faithfully discharged, will result in the unity of the nations under God, the salvation of the world through Christ, and the crown of righteousness for the faithful who enter in and enjoy the fellowship of God at the "table prepared for us."

PUNISHMENT OF THE UNFAITHFUL

Over against the rewards of faithfulness the parable places the punishment of the unfaithful. The fellow who had got two hundred and fifty pounds comes to render his account of stewardship. He has gained nothing, and has some pretty hard things to say about the master who had been away on his trip abroad. Granting, or rather waiving, the charges, the master of the unfaithful servant metes out a series of rapidly accumulating, heavy to bear, punishments.

First, and most naturally, the servant who failed to develop his ability is punished with condemnation. He does not mince words, but calls him a "rascal," an "idle servant" or lazy man, and later, "good-for-nothing." All of this because the fellow had used, what is the smart expedient of the modern church member, the plan of hoarding a talent intact, as good as new, because never used. Out from the presence of the master, the servant went branded with some hard names and forever bearing the shame of failure and forever remembering the disappointment of one who had trusted him. Could he forget what was said to the others who had preceded him in rendering accounts of stewardship? Neither could he forget his own bitter condemnation.

Second, he was punished by decrease and loss of capacity. Jesus is telling a story about capacities—let us not forget that. And the story says that when the master of the idle servant, who hid his lord's money, had finished with his denunciation of him, he commanded that the talent should be taken away from him. Without getting into any theological argument as to what is meant in transferring the talent to the man who already had twelve, let us get this lesson—that abilities, capabilities, and inherent capacities are sure to atrophy when hidden, allowed to lie idle, or when abused. We are all familiar with this principle in the matter of the physical body, of the mental faculties, and of social gifts. The tragedy of the Church of Jesus Christ consists in the willful neglect of spiritual gifts on the part of the one-talent members. These members composed the vast majority of the churches. We are witnessing alarming failures to advance in the winning of souls, in the giving of money, in the consecration of life and the inner growth of the Church because God's plain people, God's great common people, thoroughly alert in other relations, are "idle servants" in the use of their spiritual capacities.

Third, the one-talent man was punished with expulsion from fellowship. While the others were put in charge of larger sums, their capacities enlarged, and the fellowship enriched by becoming partners with the master of the story, this fellow—this rascal, lazy man, and good-for-nothing servant—was expelled from the presence of his lord. What punishment could be more severe to the Christian to-day, hungry for friends, depending for his very daily living on the fellowship and kindness of his fellow-men, than to lose the fellowship of the infinite God because he neglects, or hides, or refuses to use the capacities for devotion, for worship, for work, and for giving that is embedded in his heart as a gift from the Master of all mankind? Such a man moves perhaps in the highest intellectual circles, leads the social group of which he is a member, is unquestioned in his moral life and attitude. But he sits in the pew of his Church on the Sabbath day, isolated, lonely, and heartsick. He has expelled himself from the fellowship with God by hiding his spiritual gifts in the earth of this present life. Perhaps the channel is "choked" by cares of this world or riches or pride; or the soil of his heart may be hardened and his soul be calloused; or the soil may be so shallow that the sun and heat of the business day dries it up. But because there is no added spiritual ability to render in the account that he must make to his Lord, the man is automatically excluded from the great things his soul might enjoy.

Fourth, there is the condemnation of sorrow and remorse. The idle servant, the one-talent man, having had his talent taken away from him, is cast into darkness outside "where men will wail and gnash their teeth." That sounds like the place where Judas went after he had sold his Master for the price of a common slave and burst his bowels asunder. It sounds like the place in which Dives found himself, with a great gulf fixed between himself and Lazarus, while he begged for something cool. It sounds like the place pictured in the last judgment scene, when refusing even a cup of cold water in the Master's name, a visit to the prisoners, help to the needy, relief to the sick, those so doing are commanded to "depart from me, ye accursed ones, to the eternal fire which has been prepared for the devil and his angels." Picture the man, surrounded, as is the one-talent man of to-day, with opportunities for trading with his ability, deliberately hiding his one talent, or neglecting it, or abusing it, until it is taken away from him, he is isolated from companionship, and lives a life of remorse of consciece. He may have the comforts of this life, but he is miserable and poor and naked and blind. He lives a hell on earth. Thank God, he can turn again, repent of his folly and spiritual shortsightedness, and come back into favor with God, fellowship in the work of righteousness, and grow again in wisdom and in favor with God. Through his "Measure for Measure" Shakespeare says:

> "Heaven doth with us as we with torches do,
> Not light them for ourselves; for if our virtues
> Did not go forth of us, 'twere all alike
> As if we had them not. Spirits are not finely touched
> But to fine issues."

Pantomiming the Parable

At a recent young people's conference in Kentucky, Sunday afternoon was devoted to pantomiming Bible stories. Each class and clan was invited to compete for a suitable award to be given to the group adjudged best in its wordless portrayal of a story selected by the group as a result of a ballot. The award was won by a class of young men which pantomimed the Parable of the Talents. Those who witnessed it will always remember the main point of the parable. The exercises were held on the large and beautiful campus of Kentucky College for Women, a part of Center College, at Danville, Kentucky. Surrounded by a large audience, the boy who acted as master of the servants came forward, and in Oriental fashion called his servants to him. As they gave the Oriental salute and sign of obedience he gestured his story of his intention and desire for a trip abroad, imitating the leave-taking, indicating a train and sea trip, an appearance in high social circles, pleasure in companionship with others, and eagerness with which he anticipated rest and joy away from home. Then by a prearranged signal he called three from among his servants and made them overseers of his property, dividing the money according to the ability of the servants, as he thought. The boys in the class had taken care of this by selecting their largest in size to receive the twelve hundred pounds, a second-sized boy to receive the five hundred pounds, and one they called the "runt" to take the two hundred and fifty pounds.

Using crushed stone for money, the master of the servants delivered three different sized bags of stone to the three servants respectively, and then beckoned them to be gone about their business as he went out to climb in his automobile to take his trip that he had so carefully planned. Then each of the three boys went different routes across the campus—the one that had the large bag of money went to a group of boys out under a tree and began to trade with them; the one who had the second-sized bag was also seen to trade with a group of boys, representing Jews, under another tree; but the little fellow with the little bag found him a cool, shady spot under an overhanging tree, dug a hole in the ground, hid the bag of money, took out a cigarette, and after a smoke, went sound asleep. He was awakened by the sound of a trumpet, for the master of the servants had returned and was beckoning his servants to come up for an accounting. The two servants with the twelve hundred and five hundred pounds were plainly happy as they came on the run to greet their master, and as they came each bore an added bag of money equal in size to the one the master had committed to them when he took his departure. How glad they were when commended for their trading and frugality. In Oriental obeisance they expressed their appreciation to the master when he put into their care a large sum of money; but their joy was almost unbounded when they were asked to be guests of the master in the homecoming feast.

It took a second summons to get the little fellow to leave the shade of his tree, and it took several minutes for him to find the place he had hidden his money bag. Finally he came slowly into the presence of the master with a sort of brazen, don't-care expression. He refused to bow in Oriental fashion to salute his master. And when the master asked for an accounting, something that was not on the program happened, for the little fellow dropped his bag of crushed stone and it burst. Having his wits about him, the one who took the part of the master motioned a command that the servant should pick up the "money" and return it to the bag while he should hold his hand over the rent. When the talent was finally turned over to the master and carefully counted, and it was discovered that not a single penny had been added to the talent during the whole time of the master's absence, the expression first of grief, then of sorrow, and finally of condemnation that passed over the face of the master had its reflection in the countenance of the servant who was seen to hang his head in shame as the talent was taken from him and handed to another. The prearranged plan of the pantomime was that at this point, having portrayed his condemnation and anger, the master of the servants should clap his hands three times as a signal for all of the class of twenty-four boys to come running, take the little fellow out to the edge of the crowd and thus end the story. As sometimes happens, however, in the presence of crowds, the one-talent fellow took stage fright, and when the master clapped his hands and the fellow-members of his class came rushing toward him, the "runt" broke and ran, instinctively and with rabbitlike speed. The members of the class, relying on football instinct, gave chase and, after a hundred-yard dash, with a beautiful flying tackle brought the lad to earth. They then finished the story as it is literally finished, for they took him by the hands and legs and carried him to the edge of the campus and threw him across a privet hedge into "outer darkness." And you wonder who paid for the new suit of clothes, and why mothers turn gray? But the boys who took part in that story will have a stewardship lesson engraved on their memories and pictured in their brains that will follow them through life. It was clearly seen, as the parable shows, that the one-talent fellow was not condemned for doing positive wrong, but for willful neglect; not for the commission of grevious sins, but for leaving undone that which he had ability to do; not the breaking of commandments by sins of commission, but by a failure to take advantage of opportunities, and the sin of omission. Dr. George A. Butterick, in "The Parables of Our Lord," says that the one-talent man lacked imagination and courage. It would appear from recent transactions in the Stock Market that some men of the present generation have too much imagination and courage. But we won't go into that.

This is an age demanding as dangerous living as ever. Perish the thought that in piping times of peace there are no calls for heroes! Or that a man must fly the Atlantic, or swim the Channel, or win a row of cups in order to prove his courage and stamina and perseverance! Give us the man who has the courage to invest his talents in enterprises that would surely fail but for the help of God. Give us the man who dares to turn his back on the "proper" thing and take the dangerous route to happiness by the way of the Cross.

"Oh, it's easy to fight in the cause of right,
  When it's surely, steadily winning,
To nobly stand with a gallant band
  While plaudits loud are dinning.
For nothing inspires and fans the fires
  Of our noblest and best endeavor,
Like knowing success will crown our best
  And glory be ours forever.

But to stand with a few and yet be true
  To a seemingly losing cause;
To fight for the right with all our might
  With never a note of applause;
To stand like a brave in the face of a grave,
  O'erhung with the cloud of defeat,
This, this is the test of a hero—the best,
  A hero we seldom meet."

                                        —Anonymous.

Bishop Trench, in his comment on this Parable of the Talents, says that "while the Virgins are represented as waiting for their Lord, we have here the servants working for him." He adds a further contribution by suggestion that whereas the foolish virgins erred through overconfidence, the one-talent man erred through underconfidence. The indifference, the neglect, the carelessness of the one-talent Church member is surely the tragedy of the modern Church. Thomas H. Huxley has said, "It doesn't take much of a man to be a Christian, but it takes all there is of him." Defeat, failure, and unhappiness as a rule are not the result of the lack of ability, but of courage and earnestness. Paul's formula for living peaceably, "As much as lieth in you," is the formula for joy and victory and happiness in the spiritual as in the physical and financial world. It is Paul's way of insisting that we do the best we can with what we have. Notice a list of the potentialities or capabilities that we cannot afford to neglect and remain blameless:

Strength of body: Our bodies are temples of the Holy Spirit and we are commanded to glorify God in our bodies. Disabilities may be overcome, weaknesses may be corrected, and physical liabilities turned into assets by diligent use of daily exercise periods and health-building practices. To be an effective channel for the mind and spirit, the body must be kept clean and wholesome.

Discipline of mind: Christians of the present age, surrounded by free libraries, educational institutions, books, magazines, newspapers, and lectures, are compelled to close the mind completely in order to avoid development and discipline. Why not grow with the age? Why not take pride in a mind that can be put through the paces, taught to function at command, and be ready for use by the Lord in his work?

Cultivated friendships: This is one of the great unworked fields at our own door. There are underprivileged boys and girls in every community. Some of them live on the margin of the social order. Others live in the homes of the wealthy. And there are lonely men and women who need a friend. Christians may be friends for Christ, in Christ, and of Christ, and build the Kingdom by using the talent for friendship in the interest of the Church of Christ.

The talent for witnessing: In every Church there are those of good education, splendid personality, and strong character who might double their usefulness for the Kingdom of God by using their ability to witness for Christ in the places they work, the schoolroom, the social circle, the casual contacts, or by deliberately selecting some one who is not a Christian and attempting to win that one to Christ.

Consecrated time: Time is a marketable value, that may be improved, traded with, redeemed, and glorified. It takes time to be holy. It takes time to make friends, to train and discipline the mind, to witness for Christ and work for the Kingdom. But God makes us all equal before His throne in the daily bestowal of this precious thing, scheduled by years and months and weeks and days; divided into hours and minutes, and lived moment by moment. It is the thing with which we trade to increase our abilities, enlarge our potentialities, increase our capacities, multiply our capabilities, and prove our stewardship.

It would be easy to go on with the list—money, prayer, education, influence, business, housekeeping, profession, trade, and calling. Is it not apparent that he who would follow Jesus, who was always about his Father's business, and he who would win the approval of his own inner self and the commendation of his Lord, must be found "diligent in business, fervent in spirit, serving the Lord"? It is Marcus Aurelius who says:

ACCORDING TO CAPACITY

"Dig within thee, there lies the fount of good;
A fount whose waters will forever well up,
If thou but forever dig."

GETTING AT THE ROOT OF THE DIFFICULTY

Digging carefully into the thought and teaching of this Parable of the Talents, we discover that there were at least four things troubling the one-talent man and keeping him back from the rewards and blessings of his master.

First, he was paralyzed by fear. He said, "I was afraid." Readers of Basil King's great book, "The Conquest of Fear," will remember that he gives courage as the antidote to fear. The world is paralyzed to-day by fear of man, fear of machine; the employee fears the employer, the capitalist fears the laboring man, the children fear their fathers and mothers, and are in turn feared by their parents. This paralysis of fear causes people to refuse to release their potentialities and develop their capacities. As people on the western plains run to their storm cellars when the hurricane approaches, so we see industrial magnates run to the law for refuge when labor troubles arise, or the laboring man run to the refuge of his organization for fear he may be the victim of the industrial magnate. The man of the story is found in every church, fraternal order, community, and settlement to-day. He is the man who is afraid to stake his life on the great eternal verities, for fear he may lose.

Second, the one-talent man was a concealer. "I knew you were a hard man. . . . I went and hid your two hundred and fifty pounds in the earth." And thousands follow in his train, hiding their lights under a bushel, concealing precious gifts that may at the time be greatly needed in the promotion of the king's business. It is well that we point out that this parable is a denunciation of such concealment. The concealer is told that the two hundred and fifty pounds should have been kept in circulation by being placed in the bank. Too many Christians are out of circulation. Too many, although possessing small gifts, have withdrawn themselves from the "asset" column of the local church and become "liabilities." Almost every church court in every denomination faces the problem of what to do with the members who are "out of circulation." It may be that they are out of humor, out of cash, out of town, out of friends, or "out" in some other way. They are nevertheless concealing their abilities, hiding their talent, and are condemned of the Lord for being out of circulation.

Third, the one-talent man was a "rascal." Now, rascality does not always mean that the one guilty has his finger prints on the police record, his picture in the rogues' gallery, and a prison record to his discredit. This "rascal" of the story did the normal, usual, regular thing. He was doubtless respected by his fellow men, received in the best of society, and neat and attractive in appearance. He was a rascal because untrustworthy. For whereas the two faithful servants in the case were commended as excellent and trusty, this fellow was accused of rascality. He had not stolen the money committed to him, he had not gambled with it, he had not coveted it. But he had been an unfaithful steward because he hid it away, kept it out of circulation, and disappointed his master's trust in him.

Fourth, the one-talent man was lazy. He was called an "idle servant." And there was the source of his real difficulty. Doubtless it was from this that his fear arose, his concealment resulted, and his rascality ensued. Too many weak knees and listless hands are the result of laziness. It is the source of poverty of mind, of body, and of soul. The writer of Proverbs has much to say about the lazy man, some of which it may be well to repeat here for illustrative purposes and for illumination:

> "How long wilt thou sleep, O sluggard?
> When wilt thou arise out of thy sleep?
> Yet a little sleep, a little slumber,
> A little folding of the hands to sleep;
> So shall thy poverty come as one that traveleth,
> And thy want as an armed man."
>
> (Prov. 6: 9-11.)

> "The sluggard will not plow by reason of the cold;
> Therefore shall he beg in harvest, and have nothing."
> (Prov. 20: 4.)

> "I went by the field of the slothful, and
> By the vineyard of the man void of understanding;
> And, lo, it was all grown over with thorns,
> And nettles had covered the face thereof
> And the stone wall thereof was broken down."
> (Prov. 24: 30, 31.)

> "The slothful man saith, There is a lion in the way;
> A lion is in the streets.
> As the door turneth upon his hinges,
> So doth the slothful upon his bed.

The slothful hideth his hand in his bosom;
It grieveth him to bring it again to his mouth.
The sluggard is wiser in his own conceit
Than seven men that can render a reason."
(Prov. 26: 13-16.)

The writer of the Proverbs gives us an illustration of the proper use of talents in the thirtieth chapter, verses 24-28. He says:

"There be four things which are little upon the earth,
But they are exceeding wise:
The ants are a people not strong,
Yet they prepare their meat in the summer;
The conies are but a feeble folk,
Yet make they their houses in the rocks;
The locusts have no king,
Yet go they forth all of them by bands;
The spider taketh hold with her hands,
And is in kings' palaces."

What a story for the one-talent man to read—the ant with his one talent of foresight making sure of the future; the coney with his one talent for burrowing in the rocks, finding a safe refuge; the locusts with a talent for co-operation, succeeding thereby; the spider with one talent of perseverance, using her hands to hold on until she could get to where she wanted to go.

We are grateful for the one-talent man. The Lord must surely have loved the common people, as a great man has said, because he made so many of them. But this pins the one-talent man down, with his back to the mat, and will not let him up, who refuses to use his talent. Remember he is not the waster, the night prowler, the drunken man, nor the rioter that we have in mind here, but the perfectly respectable and good, perfectly normal, respected, easy-going, retiring, modest, and therefore utterly useless Church member that we are talking about. He simply fails to use what the Lord gave him to use, and that neglect is sufficient to bring down upon him the severe condemnation of the Lord. Especially severe, it seems, would be the condemnation of the idler, the lazy man, the sluggard to-day, who has such a variety of challenging opportunities to be found in the King's business, trading with his abilities and building the Kingdom of God.

Elsewhere we refer to Mary as a woman who made good use of her hour with the Lord, would not allow anything to interfere with the privilege of sitting at the feet of Jesus, and was commended for it. It is well to recall that, while Mary had chosen the better part, Martha had a most important work to do. It is entirely possible to sit at the feet of Jesus while engaged in the daily routine. Perhaps Jesus had this in mind when he referred to the fact that Martha was "troubled." In the use of the varied abilities with which they are so richly endowed, the women of our homes surely may "trade therewith" in the homes as they engage in the hardest and noblest of all professions—housekeeping. Through serving, and sewing, cooking, nursing, managing, mothering, and doing the thousand and one things that her busy day calls for, she may be found faithful in her stewardship. An English servant girl is supposed to have written this prayer, a tribute to the Martha type, and richly expressive of the household and kitchen stewardship of thousands of our noble women:

KITCHEN STEWARDSIP

"Lord of all pots and pans and things,
  Since I've no time to be a
Saint by watching late with thee,
  Or dreaming in the twilight,
Or storming heaven's gates,
  Make me a saint by getting meals
Or washing up the plates.

Although I must have Martha's hands,
  I have a Mary mind;
And when I black the boots and shoes,
  Thy sandals, Lord, I find.
I think of how they trod the earth
  Each time I scrub the floor;
Accept this meditation, Lord,
  I haven't time for more.

Warm all the kitchen with thy love
  And warm it with thy peace,
Forgive me all my worrying
  And make all my grumbling cease.
Thou who didst love to give men food
  In room or by the sea,
Accept this service that I do—
  I do it unto thee."

A Brooklyn minister was called to visit a girl who was dying, lonely and with a rude cellar as her home. She had for many years cared for a family of younger brothers and sisters following the death of her mother. Her father was a habitual drunkard, and the handicap of worry and work and disgrace finally wore the girl out and she was near the end of her life's journey. When the minister came she told him her life story and said, "I have heard that there is a man named Jesus who will take me to Him at death, to be with my mother who had already gone to Him." And the minister told her the story of Jesus, his birth, life, death, and resurrection, of Jesus's love for her and willingness to take her to Him. "But will He know me if I should go to Him?" pleaded the girl as she gave her heart to Jesus. The minister noticed the calloused and bruised hands as she raised them to her plea, and he remembered that they had gotten that way in the service of her brothers and sisters, and he said, "Yes, He will know you; just show Him your hands."

We have too many indifferent among the moderately endowed people, who, either by reason of fear or laziness, lift hands toward heaven with no callouses on them as a result of labor for the Lord. The average Church member has no scars of battle, nor "marks of the Lord Jesus" to show that he has been diligent in the service of the King of Kings.

The Message to Garcia

In April, 1898, when it was apparent that our nation was headed for an inevitable conflict with Spain, Col. Arthur Wagner, chief of the U. S. Bureau of Military Intelligence, conveyed to young Lieutenant Andrew Summers Rowan the wish of President McKinley that he seek, in the jungles of Cuba, one Lieutenant-General Calixto Garcia, insurgent Cuban leader, carry to him a

McKinley message, and ascertain the size and strength of Spanish forces.

Landing in Kingston, Jamaica, on April 23, carrier Rowan sailed toward Cuba that night on a dirty native fishing boat, and right under the eyes of the Spanish patrol, scouring the Caribbean. Lying flat on his back in the gunwale, he could hear the Spanish swagger alongside, shouting queries; and he could hear the answer of his pilot, the responses of the Spanish. Landing near Turquino Peak, he hurried as fast as he could inland. Through junglelike plantation land, infested with Spanish troops, he made his way, trusting his fate to shifty-eyed, silent natives. In the meantime war had been declared and the Spanish had heard of the carrier's presence in Cuba. One night a handful of Spaniards gained entrance to his camp and would have taken his life had not one of the natives saved his life for him instead, by standing between him and the enemy.

After nine days he found General Garcia, delivered his message, got his information, and started back for Washington. President McKinley personally congratulated him and promoted him to Lieutenant-Colonel, awarding him the Distinguished Service Cross. Of carrier Rowan, the late Elbert Hubbard said some things that are reported as having been reprinted at least forty million times. Said Hubbard: "In all this Cuban business there is one man stands out on the horizon of my memory like Mars at perihelion. Some one said to the President, 'There is a fellow by the name of Rowan who will find Garcia for you, if anybody can.' The point I wish to make is this: McKinley gave Rowan a letter to be delivered to Garcia; Rowan took the letter and did not ask, 'Where is he at?' By the Eternal, there is a man whose form should be cast in deathless bronze and the statue placed in every college of the land. It is not book-learning young men need, nor instruction about this or that, but a stiffening of the vertebra which will cause them to be loyal to a trust, to act promptly, concentrate their energies; do the thing."

What is true in the life of the nation is true in the life of the Church. Jesus, at the cost of His life, carried a message from God the Father, to a world lost in sin, but for that message of forgiveness and love. He is counting on us to be trustworthy in telling, by and through our abilities, and capabilities and capacities, the Story to others.

Nothing is so striking in the early history of America, nor so securely imbedded in her Declaration of Independence and Constitution, as the right and privilege, the secure protection, and the opportunity of development for the plain people. It is the one-talent man that comes in for most consideration in politics, commerce, and religion. He tills the fields, tends the looms and spindles, forges the metal, builds our buildings, supports the government, and maintains the Church. He it is, who either makes secure or undermines the social order and body politic, just as he is faithful or unfaithful to his trusteeship. The Parable of the Talents is a matchless challenge to the development of human abilities.

This parable is not directed at gross sinners, who waste their substance and abilities in riotous living, nor to those who deny the Lordship of Christ and his ownership of all that they have and are; but it is clearly a warning to those who hide their abilities. Christ would show us that it is not in the more or less that we receive, but in the faithfulness with which we handle and administer that which is intrusted to us that reward comes. In the November, 1930, issue of *Association Men,* the official magazine of the Y. M. C. A., Charles G. Muller sets forth the fact that the average young man, while busy earning a living, can acquire real culture. By "culture" he means knowledge of the best things in literature, painting, music, and the many other cultural branches of human endeavor. While earning a living he can acquire it, and it will help him to earn a better living. And it will stay longer with him if he gets it first-hand than if he gains it through the aid of teachers. The one talent will grow by use.

The Boy Who Started an Orphanage

Nearly sixty years ago, sitting in his father's home, an eight-year-old boy heard his father's guest for dinner, William Plummer Jacobs, tell of the great need in South Carolina for an orphanage. The boy thought of every plan to get some money to help start that orphanage. Finally he used his ability to pull fodder on the farm, a most humble ability, and he made fifty cents. He turned this fifty cents over to Dr. Jacobs with the sublime faith that it would be all that was necessary to get the work going. And it proved to be the case, for Dr. Jacobs told the story of the boy's use of his ability, his giving of the money—all he had—and his faith, far and wide throughout the State.

Sixty years later, Thornwell Orphanage at Clinton, South Carolina, with over three hundred children in its care, thousands of worthy alumni in all walks of life and a model of its class, is a monument to the faith of William P. Anderson, long a leading and well-loved citizen of Greenville, South Carolina, recently gone to his reward. He it was who, as a boy, made the first contribution of his one-talent and first money and great faith to start Thornwell Orphanage. Mr. Anderson became a leading banker and millman, and took a great interest in all civic affairs. He was superintendent of two Sunday schools, one of which was a mission school; he was always regular in attendance at all services in his church; a devoted personal worker and a liberal contributor of his money. His son, a leading minister in the State of Arkansas, says of his father: "To me the outstanding feature of his stewardship was the free and full use of his time." Here was a man who, though exceedingly generous with his money, because he was a trusty servant of the Lord in the use of his abilities, saw them grow and multiply before his eyes, thus bringing happiness and success in his own life and great blessings to others in the upbuilding of the Kingdom of God.

The novel, "Bethel," by Eli Millen, has as its hero, according to the author's statement, his own father, who is a minister in a small town in Mississippi—a father who used his courage and imagination to develop his abilities and become the type for portrayal of the plain, sincere religious people upon which the hope of American rests.

House of Stuart and Stewardship

The English name Stuart, and house of Stuart, variously spelled "Steward," "Stewart," "Steuart," and "Stuart," may be traced back to Fitzfald, a Norman who accompanied the Conqueror to England. His second son, Walter, who died in 1117, entered the service of David I, King of Scotland, who conferred on him some lands that were forfeited to the crown, and the dignity of the title, "Steward of Scotland." This title became hereditary, and his descendants bore it as a surname, some of the house later changing it to Steuart and Stuart.

For several generations the stewardship went from father to son. The third in line of the Stewards held also the title, Justiciary of Scotland. Alexander, the fourth Steward, was regent of Scotland during the minority of Alexander III. James, the fifth Steward, was one of six regents after the death of Alexander III. Walter, the sixth Steward, by reason of his marriage with Marjory, daughter of Robert Bruce, eventually brought the crown to the house of Steward, then called Stuart. Robert, seventh high Steward of Scotland, was regent during the captivity of David II, his uncle, and became King of Scotland when he died, taking the title Robert II.

Thus, by faithful stewardship, the House of Stuart came to the throne.

Following the death of Robert II in 1390, the Stuart succession was as follows: Robert III, James I, James II, James III, James IV, James V, Mary Stuart, James VI (who was James I as King of England), Charles I, Charles II, James VII (who as King of England, Scotland, Ireland, and France reigned as James II), Mary II, and Anne. The male line was driven from the throne during the reign of James VII (James II of England). though later the Old Pretender and the Young Pretender attempted to regain the throne for the Stuarts. After the battle of Culloden the Young Pretender's brother went to Rome and was advanced to the purple by Pope Benedict XIV, taking the title, Cardinal of York. During the French Revolution, when the Pope was driven from power, he went to Venice for refuge, aged, infirm, and reduced to poverty. George III settled an annuity of four hundred pounds on him. He died in 1807, at eigthy-two years of age, the last of the Stuarts.

The last attempt to mount the English throne by the Stuarts was made by Charles Edward Stuart, called the Young Pretender, son of the Old Pretender, James Francis Stuart. He was defeated at Culloden, and escaped to France. In 1772 he married Louise, princess of Stalberg. Because of his brutality to her, they were separated in 1780. In his latter days he lived in more or less disgrace in Florence.

It was the weak and inconsistent character of James II

that stood in the way of much-needed naval reforms during the time that he was Lord High Admiral. He went over to the Catholic religion, and on the death of his wife, and the change in national affairs, he was compelled to resign as Lord High Admiral. He was directly responsible for the famous Bloody Assize, when, led by the infamous Jeffreys, three hundred and twenty leaders were hanged. Though he hated the republicans, he was responsible for leaguing them with the regicides and the house of Stuart against the Cavaliers. He forced the elevation of the Bishop of Oxford to the presidency of Magdalen College at Oxford. He threw seven bishops in prison for disregarding the declaration of indulgences, and when it was discovered that he proposed to bring his son up in the Catholic Church, William Prince of Orange was sent for. With a force of four thousand he drove James II from the throne and saved England to Protestantism.

Fleeing to France, the deposed James II made an attempt to regain the throne, but was defeated at Boyne. During the greater part of his life he was licentious. James I, of the Stuart line, was called the "wisest fool in Christendom." It was during his reign that the King James Version of the Bible was completed (1604-11).

The story of the House of Stuart is the story repeated over and over again in family records everywhere. Faithful Stewardship, which means growth by use of abilities, brings reward and happiness; neglect, abuse, disuse, and idleness bring their own defeat, disgrace, and unhappiness. It is not by chance that the title of Lord High Steward is now used in England only on rare occasions.

"Be thou faithful unto death, and I will give thee a crown of life."

"It is required in stewards that a man be found faithful."

III

STEWARDSHIP OF TIME

PARABLE OF THE TEN VIRGINS

Matthew 25: 1-13

THEN shall the Realm of heaven be compared to ten maidens who took their lamps and went out to meet the bridegroom and the bride. Five of them were stupid and five were sensible. For although the stupid took their lamps, they took no oil with them, whereas the sensible took oil in their vessels as well as their lamps. As the bridegroom was long of coming, they all grew drowsy and went to sleep. But at midnight the cry arose, "Here is the bridegroom! Come out to meet him!" Then all the maidens rose and trimmed their lamps. The stupid said to the sensible, "Give us some of your oil, for our lamps are going out." But the sensible replied, "No, there may not be enough for us and for you. Better go to the dealers and buy for yourselves." Now while they were away buying oil, the bridegroom arrived; those maidens who were ready accompanied him to the marriage-banquet, and the door was shut. Afterwards the rest of the maidens came and said, "Oh sir, oh sir, open the door for us!" but he replied, "I tell you frankly, I do not know you." Keep on the watch then, for you know neither the day nor the hour.

(Moffatt's Translation.)

III

STEWARDSHIP OF TIME

"There is a tide in the affairs of men
Which taken at the flood leads on to fortune;
Omitted, all the voyage of their life
Is bound in shallows and in miseries.
On such a full sea are we now afloat,
And we must take the current when it serves,
Or lose our ventures."
—*Shakespeare's "Julius Cæsar," IV, iii, 216.*

THE Parable of the Ten Virgins is a story about the need for spiritual preparedness through the conservation of present time and opportunity. Andrew Fuller says, "A man only has as much religion as he can command in trial," and Dr. W. M. Taylor, in commenting on the Parable of the Ten Virgins, says that "character is revealed in crisis. It is in moments of surprise that a man's true self comes to view." We usually drift along, using just as little mental, physical, and spiritual energy as possible when suddenly, around the corner of a normal day, comes an emergency in personal life, or home life, or school life, or church life! We are forced to call upon reserves of strength. 'Tis then we realize, for the first time perhaps, that others cannot transfer to us of their oil of garnered time, conserved strength, reserve power, and spiritual preparedness. Dr. J. Newton Davies, commenting on the parable in the "Abingdon Bible Commentary," calls our attention to the need of building reserves of strength and fortitude.

We are stewards of time, the greatest capital with which we have to work in the building of the Kingdom of God, and all time is borrowed capital. The only independent capitalist in the universe is God, the "giver of every good and every perfect gift." The wise steward will take God into partnership with him as he plans, in face of life's uncertainties, to make the best possible use of his time. The point of the parable before us turns on the matter of whether or not there was reserve oil. The "stupid" had stored no reserves; the "sensible" were prepared for the emergency. Bishop Trench, in "Notes on the Parables of Our Lord," says: "By the foolish virgins are meant, not hypocrites, not self-conscious dissemblers, much less openly profane or godless, but the negligent in prayer, the slothful in work, and all those whose scheme of a Christian life is laid out rather to satisfy the eyes of men than to please him who seeth in secret." Let us lay such a measuring stick as that alongside our own Christian work and Christian living, and notice whether we are more interested on making a good impression on others with the life we now live, day by day, or whether, on the other hand, we are more interested, by practical application of the Gospel, and adequate preparation of heart, in the assurance and joys and rewards of the life to come.

STEWARDSHIP OF TIME

Now Is the Time

The present generation is being caught on the rebound by reason of a transition from the pioneer habit and training and teaching and tradition, of conquest through acquisition, to the new industrial age when industrial barons are being forced to see, if not to put into operation, the "mutual contribution" ideal of the Golden Rule. The restraining agencies of home and Church have had to combat the new feeling of dependence on scientific props brought on by the maze of machinery, contributing to a natural leaning toward the "comforts" of this present life. Now is the time to insist on the storing up of reserves of spiritual power, if in the days immediately ahead we are to enter the front door of the new order with our spiritual demands for a higher plane of business and personal living, instead of continuing to come in by the back way.

It took forty years to season Moses so that he was sufficiently prepared to lead the people of God out of the bondage of Egypt into the Land of Promise. The Exodus did not make him; it only proved that he was prepared for an emergency by knowing the source and surety of his reserve spiritual forces. A squash can be quickly grown, but it likewise quickly fades when the heat or the storm or the cold or the drought comes; while the oak, growing slowly, storing up power, stands against all emergencies of the weather. As the lighted lamp was the passport to the banquet of the bridegroom and the bride, so spiritual preparedness is the passport to life's greatest conquests. Crises never grow character; they only show it. Dr. George Hubbard in "The Teachings of Jesus in Parables" calls attention to the fact, that was fully proven in the World War, that "heroism on the battle field is often acquired in the harvest field." The battle of King's Mountain, called the turning point of the Revolutionary War, was won by boys and men who, with the native strength and patriotic ardor of men who knew only the fields and woods, had stored-up spiritual and physical strength sufficient for the emergency, and established forever their heroism. We are in the midst now, in the United States, of the finest "growing season" for producing great men that any nation has ever had, with peace perched on our banners, every possible opportunity for meditation, study, comfort, quiet, and with plenty of "proving grounds" to test our growth in clinics of the soul. But,

> "The moving finger writes, and having writ
> Moves on; nor all your piety nor wit
> Shall lure it back to cancel half a line;
> Nor all your tears wash out a word of it."

Sometimes it writes as it did on the wall for Belshazzar, "Thou art weighed in the balances, and art found wanting"; again as to Enoch who "was not, for God took him"; or as to Judas, who, breaking spiritually in the test, betrayed his Lord and "went to his own place"; or of Stephen who could pray for his enemies as he gave up his life; or of Paul who after three years in Arabia came to his work able to meet any emergency. Now is the time for us to let God write over the old, a new record that

94

covers it up in the spiritual activities of a new and better day.

LIVING ON TWENTY-FOUR HOURS A DAY

Time, the most valuable thing a man has, comes to every one as the free gift of God. We cannot borrow a minute from to-morrow or call back a moment from yesterday. With time we can build a healthy body, restore reputation, recoup fortunes, restore strength, and, with God's help, regain character. In the amount of time that God bestows he makes the ruler and the subject alike, rich in the possession of twenty-four golden hours every day. The difference in standing as among people is largely a difference in what people have done with the twenty-four hours God has given day by day in the past, and is giving now. The greatest problem that faces the Christian concerns his handling of the day. One of the most helpful books to be had on this subject is "How to Live on Twenty-Four Hours a Day," by Arnold Bennett. His thesis, that it is possible to learn to live and like to live on twenty-four hours a day, is exceedingly helpful in this day of regimentation, when the "lock-step" requirements of conformity and uniformity have tended to crush the life out of the creative element in the social order. Arnold Bennett, among many others, presents the following arresting thoughts on this matter of the stewardship of time:

1. That the average business man is running at far below his maximum horsepower, and that he puts just as

little as he possibly can into his business, and at the same time keep the wolf away from the door.

2. That it is less disastrous for a man to waste the eight hours he puts into his business than to waste the sixteen hours he has at his disposal outside of office hours and work-day hours.

3. That the best way to exceed a formal program, and get out of the routine, and really live the life of fun and health, is to get up earlier in the morning; that you can accomplish more in one morning hour than in two evening hours.

4. That since there is no aristocracy of wealth in the matter of time-supply, genius is never awarded by extra hours a day; and though you waste this precious commodity, the fresh supply of a new day is never withheld from you.

5. That in the majority of the people who really wish to live beyond the routine and humdrum, and seek to exceed the daily program of activities, this desire takes a turn toward literature.

6. That a good beginning for the novice in time-schedules is to take ninety minutes after the evening meal for three evenings a week for self-cultivation, and to build a fence of protection around them as strong as the one around the "club."

7. That one starting a program of self-improvement should start quietly and unostentatiously, because to fail in the first attempt would deal a fatal blow to self-respect.

8. That more attention should be devoted to the delicate machinery of the mind, learning to control it, channelizing it, and acquiring the power to concentrate. Get your mind in hand by the regular practice of mental exercises.

9. That we should cultivate the reflective mood in order to know ourselves and in order to see that our daily conduct is in accord with our cherished principles.

10. That we should take an interest in the arts.

11. That nothing in life is humdrum.

12. That ninety minutes reading should be followed by forty-five minutes of serious reflection.

13. That the dangers to avoid are: the danger of becoming a prig; of being tied to a program like a slave to a chariot; of developing the "rush" complex and being hurried too much; and, greatest of all dangers, the danger of failure in the beginning.

Whether we agree with these points or not—and few would count them perfect—we surely see the point of the author; that if a man is really to make a life instead of merely make a living, he must so plan the twenty-four hours of each and every day that both the working hours and the "off" hours contribute to the building up and enriching of his life, and the lives of those around him. It is well to remember that we live two days in one—the eight or ten hours of work, and the fourteen or sixteen hours away from work, at home, or engaged in recreation and methods of self-improvement. It is this "day-within-a-day" which makes or breaks character.

THIS IS THE DAY

"This is the day which the Lord hath made; we will rejoice and be glad in it." (Psalm 118:24.) The Psalmist is referring to a special day—the day when the stone which the builders had rejected had become the head of the corner. There was reason to rejoice, there was reason to be glad, there was reason to marvel, and reason to exalt and praise the Lord. It is well to remember that God instituted the idea of "special days" when we are inclined to grumble for their modern multiplicity. And yet it does seem that we are in danger of overemphasis in that respect. We have our Christmas Day, New Year's Day, Foreign Mission Day, Stewardship Day, Easter Day, Home Missions Day, Christian Education Day, Day of Prayer for Schools and Colleges, Independence Day, Labor Day, Rally Day, Thanksgiving Day, Bible Day, Orphanage Day, Music Day, and so on *ad infinitum*.

Granting the importance of these days for especial emphasis on the various phases of Kingdom development, let us remember that every day is God's day. It is hardly possible to overemphasize the religious value of observing the Sabbath day, or the importance of keeping the Fourth Commandment. But we need have no fear about the Sabbath day if we will drive home to every Christian the neglected truth that God owns every day. Every Christian who has ever tried to close God up in the Church, in order that he may not interfere in his week-day business or duties, knows with what dire spiritual consequence such attempts have always accompanied. We need to remember that the same consequences always follow the attempt to confine our work for, or worship of, God to one day in the week. The business man cannot keep God out of his business. He cannot turn out the lights, lock up the store, and say to his soul, "Now that business is over and Saturday night has come, I will prepare to serve God to-morrow." Perhaps the women are not so much tempted in this regard as are the men. There is more tendency on the part of the women to consider their home duties and their housekeeping as a holy calling than there is for the men to take their businesses as vocations to which they are called of God for seven days of the week.

We cannot much blame the women if they fail to get some of the points that are made by Arnold Bennett, because he is thinking of the business man with regular hours, with a chance to think as he goes to and fro day in and day out. It is well to remember that while "man works from sun to sun, woman's work is never done." Hers is not the privilege that comes with fixing hours and making minute schedules, but rather consists in making programs of duties to be done and then courageously cutting her cloth of duty to fit her hours and minutes of daily allotted time. Dr. W. M. MacKay in "Bible Types of Modern Women" has a valuable chapter on "A Woman of Quiet," a story of the stewardship of time as recorded in Luke 10: 38-42. He finds Mary, the woman who had the chance that day of an hour with Jesus, safely guarding that time at all odds. He finds her quiet in meditation, quiet in provocation, and quiet in consecration, as she sits at Jesus's feet. He refers to the mock quiet of some women who he considers typical of "pictureless vacuity," "cowlike placidity," and "sheeplike stupidity." One who recognizes every day as God's day will make times of quiet—the dynamic hours of every day, when power is secured to accomplish the will of God in the rest of the day. We have something to say elsewhere about the Martha type of women who, we believe, has never had a square deal, especially at the hands of the men.

How to Plan a Day

Since every day is God's day, and no man has more or less than twenty-four hours in the day, I realize that my failure or success, my happiness or distress, is largely occasioned by the use I make, by God's help, of these twenty-four hours. Therefore I will make a program of my day. It is axiomatic that "one can always do more if he will do less"; that with the multitude of things, and places, and people, and parties, and this and that and the other, crowded upon me, it is my Christian privilege and duty to sit down and count the cost for each day, selecting the things that I ought to do, or want to do, in that particular day. Time budgets are far more important than money budgets, just as time is far more valuable than money. What are some of the things which, as a Christian, I should put into my daily budget of time?

First, I will put time to worship God in every day, in private, in the family, or, at regular times of stated

100

worship in the Church, I will worship him in public. Into our laps, without money and without price, God pours every morning twenty-four golden hours. Is it not proper that we should put Him first in the day? Whether it be before breakfast or after breakfast, or at the breakfast table, every one should begin the day with worship. One man, known to the writer, realizing the rushed condition of his average day, and noticing the ease with which time for God was crowded out of the normal day, took Arnold Bennett's advice and arose an hour earlier each morning. Thirty minutes of that extra time he spent reading the Bible and in meditation; the other thirty minutes with his family. He has accomplished—and with great joy and personal satisfaction—reading the Bible through twice each year since beginning the plan. But greater than that, his whole day's work is pitched on a different and higher plane than hitherto, he gets more done at the office, and his home is happier because God is first there. Can you not see that, if God is put first in the day, he will be first all through the day?

Second, I will put time in my day for solitude. Since I came into this world alone, and must go out alone; must answer for my sins alone, and must get in touch with God alone, it is well that I cultivate the man that I must live most with—myself. How do you like to live with yourself? How many of us are literally afraid to be alone? Dr. Mel Trotter says that the cure for loneliness is to practice the presence of some person or animal with whom you can talk. The Christian always has the promise of the presence of God. He needs solitude every day, a time when he can face himself in the presence of God and "wait"—just wait upon the Lord. If we need, as Arnold Bennett insists, forty-five minutes of meditation for every ninety minutes of reading, think of how essential is solitude to the man who would "rejoice and be glad" in each and every day that God has given to him. But you say, "How can I be alone" in this machine-mad world, with something doing, somewhere to go, some one to call, or the duties of a family to interfere? The answer to that question is the task of every Christian. God says, "Be still, and know that I am God." "Stand still and I will talk with thee." "Wait." Solitude is the hardest thing in the day to secure.

Third, I will put some time in my daily program to work for God, by witnessing or service or personal testimony. There are a multitude of ways by which I may accomplish this. There are telephone calls I may make or visits to homes, or calls upon sick I may make in the interest of Christ's Kingdom. If I can sing, or talk, or teach, or heal, or preach, or speak to others in the name of Christ, there will never be lacking a multitude of daily opportunities to do Christian work. The first essential is that I be willing, and then that I deliberately set aside some part of each twenty-four hours to be used for "the Father's business." Let us remember that "we must work the works of him that sent us while it is day, for the night cometh when no man can work." Emerson once said, "Write it upon your heart that every day is the best day of the year. No man has learned anything rightly *until* he knows that every day is doomsday." And yet our policy as Christians—though we have discovered that we cannot succeed in business on such a policy—is to put off until to-morrow what we should do to-day. Hesiod divides life's day as follows: "In the morning of life, work; in the midday, give counsel; in the evening, pray." Procrastination not only steals time, it eats away at the base of character. Some active work, or witnessing or serving for God in every day, will dignify, enrich, and ennoble the daily round of cares and business and help bring the Kingdom in.

Fourth, I will put time in each day for self-improvement of body, mind, and soul. Many years ago Dr. James I. Vance wrote a book, "The Young Man Foursquare," that had a wide circulation and splendid ministry among the young people of America, in which he showed the need of mental, physical, social, and spiritual development in order to live a full life—the abundant life. If your body is not one hundred per cent strong and well, if your mind is not constantly as clear as a bell, if your soul is not atuned to the best in life, it is usually because of the daily neglect of self-improvement, and the use of the haphazard "catch-as-catch-can" idea of being "exposed" to development. Some one has said that "thirty minutes' swimming each day will keep the weight down and the morale up." Apply the same idea to other phases of development; notice that a man who will set aside one hour out of each twenty-four can read the Bible, the whole of Shakespeare, and fifty new books within the space of a year, thus improving mind, soul, and morals.

Fifth, I will put some time in my daily program for making and keeping friendships. Life can be greatly enriched, happiness increased, and the Kingdom advanced through friendships. We have seen that the story of the Good Samaritan is the master illustration of the fine art of making neighbors. Almost at the door of anyone who reads this, there are thousands of opportunities to make friends, neighbors, and Christians among the underprivileged. "If we do good to them that do good to us, what thanks have we?" We cannot afford to allow our personal friendships to get into a state of bad repair, but we must remember those in the highways and byways needing the touch of a loving hand, the word of cheer, the companionship of those who have discovered that in friendships, as in finance, "it is more blessed to give than to receive."

BUILDING A FENCE AROUND MY DAY

We have talked in terms of a most ambitious daily program. We take it for granted that the one who seeks to budget his day will put time in for eating, sleeping, working, housekeeping, study, and the normal run of daily duties. You will notice that we have talked about five things that most of us leave to chance or to one day in the week, but all of which are absolutely essential if one would live the abundant life each day. Now let us consider three failures in daily time budgets, and how to build a fence around the daily schedule so that we can protect the day for God, for ourselves, and for others.

The first common mistake among those starting time budgets is the failure to recognize each day as a new day. Oh, perhaps they turn over the page of the calendar, they do know that it is Monday, or Tuesday, or Wednesday, or Thursday. But they start out the new day just as if it were a continuation of yesterday, making the same mistakes, yielding to the same vexations, losing their tempers over the same difficulties as yesterday. Why not forget yesterday's failures and lost opportunities, face the new duties, new problems, new opportunities of a new day by saying, "This is the day which the Lord hath made." The late Senator John James Ingalls once pictured Opportunity as knocking once at every gate. Those who doubt or hesitate are condemned to failure; for however much they may seek thereafter, opportunity answers not nor returns. The matchless poem of Judge Walter Malone's is a good answer to such a sentiment and a great encouragement to that man who failed on the day before with his Christian schedule for the wise use of time:

> "They do me wrong who say I come no more
>   When once I knock and fail to find you in;
> For every day I stand outside your door
>   And bid you wake, and rise to fight and win.
>
> Wail not for precious chances passed away!
>   Weep not for golden ages on the wane!
> Each night I burn the records of the day—
>   At sunrise every soul is born again!

105

Dost thou behold thy lost youth all aghast?
　Dost reel from righteous retribution's blow?
Then turn from the blotted archives of the past
　And find the future's pages white as snow.

Art thou a mourner? Rouse thee from thy spell;
　Art thou a sinner? Sins may be forgiven;
Each morning gives thee wings to flee from hell,
　Each night a star to guide thy feet to heaven.

Laugh like a boy at splendors that have sped,
　To vanished joys be blind and deaf and dumb;
My judgments seal the dead past with the dead,
　But never bind a moment yet to come.

Though deep in mire, wring not your hands and weep;
　I lend my arm to all who say 'I can.'
No shamefaced outcast ever sank so deep,
　But yet might rise again and be a man!"

To the one who will take time by the forelock each day, and every day, this matter of "exceeding the program" becomes a happy game; and with the gift of time, comes the gift of physical, moral, and spiritual courage sufficient unto the day.

The second failure in the matter of daily time budgets is the failure to make the schedule fit the individual. It is impossible for another to make a satisfactory daily schedule for me. And yet how often we witness such schedules being made in conference! Consultations with members of the family, friends, and business associates is most valuable, but the fact cannot be too strongly emphasized that each soul stands alone and as a unit before God, and that to get the most out of a day, avoid failure, and get joy we must each fix his or her own program of hours and minutes to fit each individual case.

The third reason for failure in time budgets is in the failure to master the budget, but instead letting the budget master us. Like Atlas with the world on his back, we go through the day rushed and driven like dumb cattle because we want to live according to a budget. The man is a fool that will let a machine that he has erected, the creation of his own brain and soul, turn and rend him, crushing out his joy, his spontaneity, and his success. It is necessary to remember that a budget will not work automatically; that it is not something that will be lying by us upon a silver platter each morning when we get out of bed. God gives us the day. He expects us to have sense enough, judgment enough, and trust in Him enough, to take this matchless gift of his and, by fitting each day's duties into each day's hours, so change the program from day to day as to come to the close of each day rejoicing and glad. There is a vast difference in being on top of a budget and being caught underneath it and being mastered by it.

REDEEMING THE TIME

Getting back to the Parable of the Ten Virgins, let us notice that it was not until their reserve supply of oil was depleted that the "stupid" maidens were made aware of the preciousness of time. Then it was that they learned that time is not a transferable element of life and reserves were invaluable. If they have time now, however, they will go buy! If they have time, they will still go into the banquet! If they have time, they will yet get back before the door of opportunity is shut! If they have time! But when they returned, they found that the bridegroom had come, the banquet was on, and the door was shut! Here is Tennyson's picture:

> "Late, late, so late! and dark the night, and chill!
> Late, late, so late! but we can enter still.
>   'Too late, too late! Ye cannot enter now.'
>
> No light had we; for that we do repent;
> And learning this, the bridgroom will relent.
>   'Too late, too late! Ye cannot enter now.'
>
> No light! so late! and dark and chill the night—
> Oh let us in, that we may find the light.
>   'Too late, too late! Ye cannot enter now.'
>
> Have we not heard the bridegroom is so sweet?
> Oh let us in, though late, to kiss his feet!
>   'Too late, too late! Ye cannot enter now.' "

Let us notice, from among the hundreds of references in the Bible on the importance of time and the value of conserving and redeeming it, particularly the following:

"See then that ye walk circumspectly, not as fools but as wise, Redeeming the time, because the days are evil."

(Eph. 5: 15, 16.)

"To everything there is a season, and a time to every purpose under heaven." (Eccles. 3: 1.)

"Remember now thy Creator in the days of thy youth, while the evil days come not, nor the years draw nigh, when thou shalt say, I have no pleasure in them." (Eccles. 12: 1.)

"So teach us to number our days, that we may apply our hearts unto wisdom." (Ps. 90: 12.)

STEWARDSHIP OF TIME

"Sow to yourselves in righteousness, reap in mercy;
Break up your fallow ground;
For it is time to seek the Lord,
Till he come and rain righteousness upon you."

(Hosea 10: 12.)

"The night is far spent, the day is at hand:
Let us therefore cast off the works of darkness,
And let us put on the armor of light."

(Rom. 13: 12.)

There are many ways by which we may "redeem" the time. We may buy it up by giving less time to the things that are of least importance and more time to the things that are most important. We may buy it back by taking it from the places and people where it is being squandered and putting it on the themes, and things, and people where it will be conserved. By faithfulness, energy, zeal, and well-doing we may use it to store up reserves of physical and mental and moral and spiritual power. By study, preparation, prayer, and Christian application to the duties of the day immediately before me I may so "number my days as to apply my heart" unto the wisdom of Christian growth, and happiness, and contentment. The best time of each day should be used for the most difficult tasks. By taking time by the forelock rather than being dragged at the chariot wheels of the day I shall be a faithful steward.

When Borden of Yale '09 died in Egypt, on his way to the foreign mission fields, he left behind a great fortune of more than a million dollars to continue his work as a steward of Christ after he could no longer serve Him. Borden's chief concern, in college, traveling in the interest of the Volunteer Movement, assisting in rescue mission work, or wherever he served, was that he should make the best use of his time. He is the outstanding illustration to young people, standing on the brink of their life decisions, of one who, during his college days, put the emphasis on the spiritual values of life. Undoubtedly, if his biographers are near the truth, he is the modern illustration of the rich young man who, instead of turning away from Jesus with sorrow, turned to Jesus, renouncing his all, giving it away in his will, becoming one of Jesus's modern disciples. Listen to him, while a sophomore at Yale, as he talks to us through his diary: "I figured up yesterday where my time went per week and found that about thirty-five hours are wasted somehow. I am going to see if I can't systematize so as to get the most use out of them."

Not long ago Sidney Smith, with his inimitable "The Gumps," gave us one of the greatest sermons on the stewardship of time to be found anywhere. He pictures Father Time announcing to Andy Gump, as he lies asleep, the coming of a new day. The day, big and strong, excellent in body and radiant with happiness, comes in and says: "I am the day—I have come with my twelve little men, the hours; they are here to work for you. They work untiringly, willingly, and freely—you have but to command them." Then in succession, forth from the dial of a great clock, step little uniformed men, each in a different uniform, representing the hours of the day, placing themselves at Andy's command. Finally, all of the hours having passed in review before him, the day comes to a close and Father Time returns bearing the scythe and the hourglass. The day is reaped into eternity's garner and those hours will never return:

> "To-morrow I will live, the fool does say,
> To-day itself's too late,
> The wise lived yesterday."

You can imagine Andy Gump's relief, when he awoke and discovered that this story of the loss of a day was a dream, and his consequent determination not to let a moment get away that failed to record some useful task accomplished. It was this same Andy Gump, with a sudden flair for figures, who calculated that if he would get up each morning at five instead of eight o'clock, in one year he would add 1,095 hours to his life, in ten years 10,950 hours, in forty years 43,800 hours—and that, figuring on a twelve-hour basis, he would add 3,650 days or ten years to his life of real living! Think that through!

Triple Reserves

Mr. Roger W. Babson in his excellent and helpful book, "Storing Up Triple Reserves," establishes the theme of the Parable of the Virgins by showing that men are made or marred in emergencies, so far as the public estimate is concerned, but that this public making or marring in crises depends upon the sufficiency or insufficiency of physical, financial, and moral reserves. It was overanxiety that Jesus condemned, and not thrift. It was the setting of the heart on riches for the sake of riches, and the false reliance on the material things of life, that Jesus condemned. Jesus did not condemn the physical appetite, but the abuse of it, or reliance on it, or the worship of it. By the observance of proper hours, by the diligent participation in certain exercises, by wise bathing and the proper care of the body, powerful physical reserves can be stored. It takes time to be healthy. Mr. Babson and Mr. Franklin Roosevelt are outstanding and commanding illustrations of what physical exercise and wise stewardship of the body will do to restore, as well as to conserve health. Prosperity, health, and contentment come at a price—the price of honest, simple, healthful, scheduled daily living.

Mr. Babson assigns four reasons for worry: ill health, poor education, too little money, and poverty of faith. All of these are occasioned by failure of reserves upon which one may draw. Over against these, he lists man's chief assets—faith, family, friends, and funds. Over against railroads, and factories, and farms he lists sympathy and hope and courage as the greatest things in the world. These last are spiritual resources. It takes time to store them, but a reserve supply of them makes a man undefeatable in the battles of life. To the man or woman, the city, the home, the state, the church which takes time to store up such reserves of strength, these become tools with which to work. Right hearts precede right laws and right homes. Jesus warned against a life, surfeited with food, shelter, clothing, and luxuries, while the soul starves for the search and sight of the Kingdom of God. The only way to be ready for the Bridegroom is to be sure of our reserve supply of oil. It takes time to be holy, but it is holiness alone that will stand the test in that Day. It is this same Mr. Babson who is quoted in the news dispatches as laying the blame of the great stock debacle in 1929, and the depression in 1930, on the collapse of character. In a financial emergency the spiritual and moral reserve was insufficient to stand the test. Here is an interesting coincident; just as the writer had pounded out the preceding sentence on his typewriter a card, sent out by the local Y. M. C. A. and signed "Roger W. Babson," was laid on his desk. The card states: "Business depressions are caused by dissipation, dishonesty, disobedience to God's will—a general collapse of moral character. Statistics show this plainly. With equal precision they show how business depressions are cured. They are cured by moral awakening, spiritual revival, and the rehabilitation of righteousness." What is this but a call for the mobilization of reserves? How distressing if they are not available for such mobilization and consequent use!

The disconcerting thing about life's emergencies is that we can never anticipate them. It may be a case of unusual and unforeseen temptation, accident, death of a loved one, pestilence, failure of fortune, betrayal by friends, or collapse of most cherished dreams. But by carefully scheduling his time, and wisely building into his plans for each day, the steward may store away reserves. With the brick and mortar of a noble life, he may build on the eternal Rock, so that when the storms descend and the rains fall, he stands secure and unmoved. Of the late Senator Henry Gassaway Davis it is said, on the equestrian statue erected to him at Charleston, West Virginia:

> "He worked as though he would live forever,
> He lived as though he would die to-morrow."

Contrast this with the statement of Epicurus, "The business of most men in my day was a madness, and their rest a lethargy"—a statement which is all too true of the "tired" business men to-day. "Keep on the watch," said the Master, for "you know neither the day nor the hour." Sounding as though they were written for this very day are the following lines from James Russell Lowell's "The Present Crisis":

"New occasions teach new duties, time makes ancient good uncouth;
  They must upward still and onward, who would keep abreast of truth."

Or these from Henry Wadsworth Longfellow's immortal "Psalm of Life":

> "Art is long, and time is fleeting,
>   And our hearts, though stout and brave,
>   Still like muffled drums are beating
>   Funeral marches to the grave."

CAN A HOUSEKEEPER BUDGET HER TIME?

Lest we be accused of thinking of time schedules in terms of the business man who observes office hours, and should find it easy to make and exceed daily programs for his life, let us address ourselves to those real makers of civilization, the housekeepers and home-makers. According to a report in the newspapers, Secretary of Labor Davis called the wife of the workingman "the greatest, busiest business executive in the world." "There is a real rock-ribbed, hide-bound working schedule under the surface of the weekly household activities," he said. "Each day has its special tasks which must be performed with clocklike regularity. Monday is washday; Tuesday, ironing; Wednesday is for mending and sewing; Thursday is for odd jobs like making jelly and mending the furniture; Friday is cleaning day; Saturday is the biggest day of all, with cooking and catering, and attending to children coming home from school; and Sunday is no day of rest for her." We agree with Secretary Davis, that the job of feeding and clothing a family of eight, including several growing boys and a husband, is almost enough to dishearten anyone. But the working wife tackles the job like a football hero. She may get tired and cross and worn and weary. But why shouldn't she? Look at her tasks—wife, mother, nurse, housekeeper, cook, laundress, seamstress, shopper, financier, and home-maker! Think of her—and admire her you must—as we ask the question, Can a housekeeper follow a program or time schedule? It seems that such a question is already answered in the catalogue of her duties just recited. Surely if she is to get rid of being a slave, driven to her arduous duties; if she is to substitute the joy of home-making for the drudgery

115

of housekeeping, and child-training or child-management, she must find some way to master her hours rather than be mastered by them. Or let us answer the question this way: the housekeeper should build her daily program around themes rather than things. There are some things she "must" do every day, and always there are a multitude of things she "wants" to do. The things she wants to do concern the great themes of life, such as making friendships, Christian work, worship, service, and Christian self-improvement. If "the hand that rocks the cradle rules the world," and the world is to be saved for the Kingdom of God, the housekeeper and home-maker must so arrange her day, given to her of God, that time is set aside for the cultivation and the inculcation of the great character-making themes.

How One Woman Did It

A great story of how one busy housekeeper used her time is that told us by Josiah Gilbert Holland in "The Mistress of the Manse." It is the story of the wife of a pastor, trying hard to find her place in the daily life of a minister. One day, alone in her husband's study, surrounded by his books, that she had once thought she would master in order to keep pace with her husband, she faced the whole matter of her life and her daily schedule with her Master. She decided that, in addition to her regular household duties, she should become a complement to her husband in his great work, that she should do the things that she was best fitted to do. Her first work was to take a needy child and make her happy. Then she found the six brothers and sisters of that child, solicited food and clothing for them; and then one bright Sunday morning, with the courage of a hero, marched into the church bringing the whole brood to hear her husband preach of Christ. Her reputation for this kind of work grew, her sympathy for the neglected became contagious, and men, women, and children made a pathway to her home for help and guidance. She lifted a great load off of her husband, fulfilled her own ambition to do something outside the daily grind, and became master of her time. After her husband's tragic death in the War between the States, she lived to see her own son occupy the pulpit of his father, while she remained the mistress of the manse, mender of broken hearts, and trustee of her opportunities.

THE STEPS TO TAKE

No two people can live on the same time budget, and it is unwise to presume that we may here make a schedule that would be foolproof or air-tight. But we can suggest steps in making a daily time budget which have proved helpful to all who have ever followed them.

First, draw a circle representing twenty-four hours, and divide the circle into twenty-four equal segments. Each segment will represent an hour. Take a page of plain white paper and draw a line down the center. On the upper left put down "assets" or "receipts"—24 hours —and on the upper right, "disbursements" or "expenditures." Remember, a budget is an estimate of how much

117

you expect to receive and what you expect to do with it after you get it. The circle of twenty-four hours represents your receipts for the day. God gives to all alike, no more, no less than a full day. Having gone this far, we are prepared to begin to list our probable expenditure of time each day.

Second, put down the things that you know must be done each day, such as sleeping eight hours, working eight hours, dressing and eating two hours, and recreation two hours. This may be called the process of elimination in getting at a real program for the day. By this process we have now spent twenty hours.

Third, list the things that you really would like to do each day. Among them will be self-improvement, worship and devotion, work for God, friendships and Christian fellowship. These are themes around which you will need to build your day-within-the-day, varying the time allotted to them day by day. But remember they will never be put in the time schedule unless you put them there.

Fourth, go back now to the circle of twenty-four hours, begin with the time you get up in the morning, say seven o'clock, and fit all of the things you must do and want to do into the hours of the segmented circle, and presto! you have a budget! Remember it is easy to make a time budget. It is hard to keep one. Nothing is more tragic than a life that is being ridden or driven by a schedule, a system, a scheme; failing to "rejoice and be glad" in the day the Lord has given for our enjoyment. Man's chief

118

end, according to one Church catechism, is to "enjoy" God as well as to glorify Him. Those pursuing this idea of time budgets will find much help in "The Larger Stewardship," by Charles A. Cook (Chapter VII); "Studies in Stewardship," by R. P. Anderson, (Chapter IV); "Woman and Stewardship," by Ellen Quick Pearce (Study IV); "Stewardship in the Life of Women," by Helen Kingsbury Wallace (Chapter IV); and "Life as a Stewardship," by Morrill (Chapter III).

How a Rich Steward Used His Time

One of the outstanding laymen in contemporary Church history was the late George W. Watts, of Durham, North Carolina, philanthropist, church leader, and steward of life and time, who, after making rich investments of his personality in the Kingdom of God, went to his reward in 1921 at the age of seventy years. Trained in the public schools of Baltimore and later at the University of Virginia, he so garnered his time and harnessed it to his ideals that by the time he entered business as a salesman for his father's firm he was recognized as possessing qualities which foretokened success. At the age of twenty-seven years he began his business career with W. Duke Sons and Company in Durham. At the same time he began to be a creative force in the business world, a public-spirited community builder, leader of civic progress, an open-handed philanthropist, and an exemplary Christian, seeking first the interests of the Kingdom of God.

He so controlled his time that he was present at every

service of his church, not only on Sunday but during the week, unless providentially hindered. For over thirty years he superintended the Sunday school of his Church. He gave freely of his time in mission work, and for a long period of years went down every Sunday afternoon, fair or foul weather, and taught a Bible class at one of the mills, and every Friday night he conducted the services at the same mill. As his influence and reputation spread he was made trustee of many institutions, and asked to serve on committees and agencies of the various church courts of which he was a member. When he attended meetings of church courts or committees or agencies, because he set aside the time for the whole meeting, he always arrived on time, and always stayed through to the end of the sessions. It was largely his interest and money that made possible the moving of Union Theological Seminary to Richmond, Virginia, from its former location at Hampden Sidney, and the making of it one of the great seminaries of the nation. Its main building at the new location was the gift of Mr. Watts, as also the beautiful chapel. He made numberless other gifts to its improvement and its permanent funds. He endowed the President's chair and the chair of Religious Education; he gave a large sum for supplementing inadequate salaries, and left a goodly sum in his will to continue to work for the Seminary after his death.

George W. Watts was a great steward of God. Besides his keen interest in Union Theological Seminary, he reached out to touch dozens of other institutions and enterprises, giving freely of money and personality and time to colleges, orphanages, training schools, hospitals, home and foreign mission work, Sunday school extension, and other great benevolent enterprises.

George W. Watts always gave himself with his money. There was nothing cold or detached in his giving, because his heart went with his hand. He was a man of humility and gentleness, yet of great mental grasp, swift and sure in his analysis of a need and the meeting of a need; far-visioned, but always courteous and firm. Those who served with him on boards and committees tell of the great happiness he got out of life as he devoted his time to Christian work. He was a wise counselor and a faithful trustee, whost beaming face was a constant witness of his contentment of heart when found in the service of the King of Kings.

Time for Quiet

In the path that George W. Watts trod to happiness there are thousands of others we might name. Not many of course that rendered such a full measure of devotion as did this great steward, but many who have discovered that the secret of a well-spent day and a happy life is in finding time each day to "practice the presence" of the Lord, a time of solitude, of meditation, and of devotion alone with God. No man can succeed with a time budget who does it by "main strength and awkwardness," trusting to his own ingenuity and ability. No man or woman, young man or young woman, can fail with his daily program if he or

she will put God first in His day and find time every day to
wait quietly upon the Lord.   Listen to the words of the
Psalmist, translated by Moffatt, and recorded in Psalm
62: 5-8:

> "Leave it all quietly to God, my soul,
>   My rescue comes from him alone;
> Rock, rescue, refuge, he is all to me,
>   Never shall I be overthrown.
>
> My safety and my honor rest on God;
>   God is my strong rock and refuge.
> Always rely on him, my followers,
>   Pour out your prayers to him;
>   God is a refuge for us."

Leave it all quietly to Him.

IV

THE CONQUEST OF COVETOUSNESS

PARABLE OF THE RICH FOOL
Luke 12: 13-23

A MAN out of the crowd said to him, "Teacher, tell my brother to give me my share of our inheritance"; but he said to him, "Man, who made me a judge or arbitrator over your affairs?" Then he said to them, "See and keep clear of covetousness in every shape and form, for a man's life is not part of his possessions because he has ample wealth." And he told them a parable. "A rich man's estate bore heavy crops. So he debated, 'What am I to do? I have no room to store my crops!' And he said, 'This is what I will do. I will pull down my granaries and build larger ones, where I can store all my produce and my goods. And I will say to my soul, "Soul, you have ample stores laid up for many a year; take your ease, eat, drink, and be merry."' But God said to him, 'Foolish man, this very night your soul is wanted; and who will get all you have prepared?' So fares the man who lays up treasures for himself instead of gaining the riches of God." To his disciples he said, "Therefore I tell you,

"Do not trouble about what you are to eat in life,
  Nor about what you are to put on your body;
Life is something more than food,
  And the body is something more than clothes."

(Moffatt's Translation.)

124

IV

THE CONQUEST OF COVETOUSNESS

"Good name in man and woman, dear my lord,
Is the immediate jewel of their souls:
Who steals my purse steals trash; 'tis something, nothing;
'Twas mine, 'tis his, and has been slave to thousands;
But he that filches from me my good name
Robs me of that which not enriches him
And makes me poor indeed."
                    —*Shakespeare's "Othello," III, iii, 160.*

"How quick all nature falls to revolt,
When gold becomes her object.
We bring it to the hive,
And like the bees are murdered for our pains."
          —*Shakespeare's "King Henry IV," Part two.*

THE Parable of the Rich Fool was precipitated by a man who evidently exhibited in his demeanor the thing that was bothering him most—covetousness. He interrupted Jesus in the midst of His teachings about the way of life to seek His intervention in a matter that had to do with food and shelter and clothing. Jesus was, and is, interested in these things, but the business-type of man who thinks that everything should be sidetracked for "business interest" gets a merited rebuke in Jesus's answer to the interruption and His subsequent parable. "Covetousness," says Dr. W. M. Taylor, "is not simply the desire for, or possession of, property, but it is the desire of

125

having it simply for the sake of having it—the making of that which is a means unto an end in itself." It is putting cash above character. Covetousness is the sin which we are afraid to mention. It walks the streets, sits in the pews of the churches and on official boards with head up, unafraid and respected. And yet it takes its place in the Ten Commandments along with theft, and murder, and slander. In Paul's writing it takes its place with sexual immorality, drunkenness, and the vilest of sins. Jesus did not condemn success; he did not condemn wealth, but he did condemn the man who would try to serve both God and Mammon. Thank God for the great and growing multitude of men and women who have rid their souls of covetousness and found abundant life by serving God *with* mammon.

God's Portrait of a Fool

Here is the matchless miniature word-picture of a fool: "He layeth up treasures for himself, and is not rich toward God." His twin brother lives in every town to-day; we consult him on business affairs, we honor him with official positions, we praise him for his leadership, we call him our first citizen, borrow money from him, and put him on all official school boards, civic committees, and Church boards. If we will notice the Parable of the Rich Fool closely, we will find many things to commend in the fool:

1. He acquired his wealth honestly. There is no hint of the "bucket shop" or of gambling on the margin, or

of robbing his employees of their just wages. He was engaged in the oldest of all "producing" industries, that of farming, and with a large list of employees there was no grumbling at ill-treatment.

2. He was wise in the saving of his money. He made timely preparation against unforeseen circumstances in order to be able to take care of the future needs of his family, his farm tenants, and those connected with his business. In the days before life insurance companies he took out the best form of insurance—stored up goods, saved money, hoarded wealth for the use of emergency needs. Looking at him purely from a "business" point of view, he was a wise man.

3. Apparently he was a good spender. He is preparing to retire from business. He does not seek to corner the market, but only to put aside enough to comfortably provide for himself. His building of barns after tearing down his old ones would give lucrative employment to architects, contractors, laborers, and others; would be a good thing for the community and, while profiting him, would at the same time help business conditions.

4. He was no miser. Having secured a competence, he was willing to retire from the field of business and let others have a chance at success.

5. Having no evidence to the contrary, we presume that he was a good family man, a good neighbor, and from all outward appearances a good man—doubtless temperate, thrifty, and careful of his companionships.

And now, before this fellow gets to be so good that we

fall in love with him, and forget or overlook his defects, let us look closer at the portrait and notice the reason for his downfall, death, and condemnation at the hands of the one who paints the portrait for us:

1. He had no spiritual foresight along with his business acumen. It is the picture of character collapse in a man who thought he could retire from business with nothing but comfort and luxury to retire on. Sinclair Lewis has given us his modern type in "Dodsworth," a rich man trying to retire with nothing but money and "success" to retire on. Take the money props from under such a man and his character collapse is equal to that of the descent from the sky of a deflated balloon.

2. He thought he could feed his soul on corn and oats. He says so very frankly in a short speech he addresses to his soul. He thought that material things could take the place of spiritual themes. It is well to remember in this connection that those two, "things" and "themes," are not mutually exclusive. There is no reason why a man may not have them both in his life. Many wealthy men are great Christians.

3. He lost sight of God's ownership of his money. In making his millions he forgot the man inside. He refers to his farm produce as "my" goods, to his barns as "my" barns, and to the increase of the soil as "my" crops, while all the time he got his increase of wealth almost immediately from the hand of God—God's rain and sunshine and soil, and seasons and strength with which to get

it. From the fields to the barn or bank is the most direct route anything can come from God to man.

4. He neglected his stewardship. With bursting barns, he forgot the needy, forgot God, forgot that he owed all to Him, and thought only of "bigger and better" barns. He forgot that bare homes, hospitals, and charitable institutions are better places than bank vaults for the purpose of safe-keeping and investment of surplus goods.

5. He was a covetous man. It was to show that fact that Jesus gave us his picture. He traded his opportunity to help the needy, his obedience to Christian ideals, joy in service and glorious philanthropy, for barns and goods, and threw his soul in for good measure. He could not distinguish between life and livelihood, between "mine" and "thine," or between God and gold. He did not possess his possessions—they possessed him, dominated him, and destroyed him. When separated from the world of "goods" upon which he had come to depend, he had no riches within his soul upon which to rely. Therein lies the tragedy of his death. Listen again to the "prosperity" speech this covetous man made on the night of his death: "What am *I* to do? *I* have no room to store *my* crops. . . . This is what *I* will do. *I* will pull down *my* granaries and build larger ones, where *I* can store all of *my* produce and *my* goods. And *I* will say to *my* soul, 'Soul, you have ample stores laid up for many a year; take your ease, eat, drink, and be merry.' "

This Year's Model

"Take heed and beware," said Jesus! But this year's model of the rich fool, caught as he is, in the grip of an acquisitive social order, refuses to believe that the accumulation of "things" without growth of the soul is suicidal; refuses to believe that a "man's life is not a part of his possessions because he has ample wealth," and blindly attempts to buy happiness, character, health, and usefulness with money. Lest we turn this discussion toward men of six-figure incomes, suppose we make a list of the things the citizen of to-day of America's "Middletowns" is most interested in. It will read: food, shelter, clothing, comforts, luxuries, education, social position, and enjoyment of things that may be had for a material consideration. Over against the great challenges to missionary endeavor, philanthropy, and investments in character-building we place our program of bigger and better barns. Although we know that "he that winneth souls is wise" and that we can transmute our money into saved souls, we steadfastly hold on to the comforts of life; we continue to make purses that wax old and lay up treasures on earth rather than in heaven. Dr. Marcus Dods, in "The Parables of Our Lord," says: "A man often measures himself by what he has instead of by what he is. He may fill his shelves with the wisest and most elevating books, and yet remain illiterate; he may gather around him precious works of art and be a clown or a boor; he may buy up a county and be the smallest-souled man in it; he may erect a mansion which will last for ten generations, and may not have ten years of life or ten minutes of health to enjoy it. A man's possessions obstinately stand off from him." And yet the man of to-day refuses to see it that way, and continues the accumulation of things, thinking thereby and therewith to feed his soul.

The man who touched off the parable before us thought he could use Jesus as a referee in a contested will. That is how much he appreciated the mission of Jesus. We are familiar with the man "having the gold ring on" who uses the Church of Jesus Christ as the stepping-stone to his material ends. This kind of man in his ruthless pursuit of success merely for the sake of success, of wealth just to have wealth, or position for the sake of position; who forgets that these should be used as a means to an end rather than as an end in themselves—this man is the modern type of the Bible Fool. He ignores God, ignores his fellow men except to use them, ignores his own soul's interests by thinking to feed it with silver and gold, and ignores the real meaning of life. The Greek language has two words for our word "life": one meaning the life that we live—natural life; and the other meaning the life by which we live—the spiritual life. It is significant that accumulated possessions can sustain neither the physical life here nor the life of peace, joy, happiness, and immortality. They are both outside and beyond sustentation by mere money. Possessions may aid life, or they may hinder, strangle, harass, and depress life; but they cannot produce life, nor when the time has come for death to reap his harvest, can possessions alone sustain life.

Augustine tells the story of a man spending the night with a friend, and, discovering that the friend's fruit was rotting in a low damp room, suggested that he move it up to a higher room. This was done and the fruit was saved. What we need most to-day is to raise our rotting riches to a higher room, to lay up for ourselves in heaven, thus avoiding the moths and the rust and the wear and tear of the modern program for bigger and better barns. Fannie Hurst, in her novel "Five and Ten," has John G. Rarick, the "Dodsworth" of her story, to say, near the close of his life, after he had lost his wife by death, his only son by suicide, and was left with an only daughter, who was a stranger to him: "I am worth $180,000,000; and yet, personally, I have never succeeded." At sixty years of age Rarick set himself to the new and better job of giving away all of his money in honest ways, and then hoping that he might die poor but successful.

"Dollars Only"

Beneath the Singing Tower at Lake Wales, Florida, rest the mortal remains of Edward Bok, editor, author, business man, and philanthropist. He came to this country as an immigrant boy from the Netherlands, carved out for himself a name, a career, and a success; a position in public life and a reputation for personal success, such as few native-born Americans have achieved. He held the theory—and lived it—that a man's success in life should be divided into three periods: the period of education, the period of achievement, and the period of retirement from active business in order to help his community. He was office boy for a telegraph company at thirteen, when he was forced to quit school to support others; editor at nineteen, and editor of the *Ladies' Home Journal* at twenty-five. About a decade ago he retired from active work in order to enjoy life and help others to enjoy it with him. He began immediately to illustrate and improve his stewardship of life, time, talents, and money. Among his outstanding accomplishments are: (1) Authorship of "Two Persons," "A Man from Maine," "Twice Thirty," "The Young Man in Business," "The Young Man and the Church," "The Americanization of Edward Bok," and "Dollars Only," all widely read and spiritually helpful books—a list that would establish any man as a success in life had he done nothing else. (2) He established the $100,000 Peace Prize for the American who can advance the "best practical plan by which the United States may coöperate with other nations to attain and preserve world peace." (3) He created a public award of $10,000 to be given annually to the person who shall perform the outstanding single act calculated to best promote the interests of the city of Philadelphia. (4) He made possible the Philadelphia Forum, a benefit to teachers and others of limited means, providing an extensive list of lectures, entertainments, and concerts at a nominal sum. (5) For five years he was the unknown donor of $250,000 annually to make up the deficit sustained by Philadelphia orchestra. (6) He created eight annual awards consisting of a gold medal and a purse of $8,500 to promote better newspaper and periodical advertising in the United States and Canada. (7) He established the Philadelphia Citizen's Award whereby each year the three policemen, three firemen, and three Fairmount Park guards performing the most meritorious acts receive each $1,000. (8) He built the famous "Bok Singing Tower" and created a bird sanctuary at Lake Wales, Florida. Because "his heart was there" it was to Lake Wales he went in his last illness. It was there he rendered to his Maker the final account of his stewardship of life, and there his body rests to-day.

Late in his life Mr. Bok said, as he was quoted in the newspapers: "The realization is growing that ledgers of the counting room do not always and exclusively mark the progress of the world." It was his spiritual conviction that the world could never be put in the straight jacket of business and finance. He believed that if we make business our king, then we will make gold our God. His whole life is a glorious protest against the philosophy of the Rich Fool of Jesus's parable and his 1931 counterpart; against the twentieth century's chief temptation and chief spiritual danger of putting economics before ethics, and gold before God. In 1926 he gave to the world one of the finest of stewardship books to be found in the growing library on that subject. The book is "Dollars Only." In it he insists that the wisest forms of wealth that a man can lay up are expenditures for and investments in development of character; that there should come a time in every man's life when he quits the chase after the things he can get out of life and begins to think of what he can put into life; that the possession of wealth and the ability to accumulate it must be regarded as a stewardship; that private means are a public trust, not something for a man to have and to hold, but a stewardship that he has and gives; that "A good name is rather to be chosen than great riches, and loving favor than silver and gold"; that a man who goes out of this life, leaving a great fortune for his family alone, perpetuating his own name simply by the money he leaves, is not in line with a growing, healthy, American sentiment; and finally he insists that with all his getting, a man should take time to get acquainted with his soul before it leaves his body. May the lengthened and strengthened shadow of this great steward, who found a place to store his "goods" in the hearts of his fellow men, fall with mighty power and influence upon this world of ours!

Stewardship Standards

Let us get at the principles which the Rich Fool violated, thereby bringing down upon himself the condemnation of the Master and summary death. Among the many others there are four fundamental guideposts on the route to Christian Stewardship:

1. God is the owner. "The earth is the Lord's, and the fullness thereof, the world, and they that dwell therein." There are a multitude of references that might be adduced to show that God has never released His ownership of the world and all that is in it or of it or on it. "In the begin-

ning God created" every living thing including man, and he gave man dominion or a lease for life. It is easy to show a child God's ownership by tracing back the kiddy car, or chair, or toy to the tree or earth and the God who made all things. The Rich Fool and the poor fool, alike to-day, refuse to remember the things they learned when the first question in the little catechism was asked in Sunday school, "Who made you?" was easily answered, "God." All other answers follow—that God made all things; that He made them for His own glory, and so on.

2. Man owes. He owes to God his life, his time, his abilities, his money—his all. God's Word for it is, "So every one of us shall give an account of himself to God." (Rom. 14: 12.) If we must give account, then the things that we have of life and possessions do not belong to us, but to God. They are his by right of creation, redemption, and preservation. Man is a possessor, never the owner of his money. He owes it all to God; God asks him to remember that fact. We owe God our bodies, our personalities, our minds, our hearts, our heads, our hands. We are mere tenants, caring for another's property. Our care of it should be such that we are ready at any and all times to render account of our stewardship.

3. Man should honor God with his money. "Honor the Lord with thy substance, and with the first fruits of all thine increase; so shall thy barns be filled with plenty, and thy presses shall burst out with new wine." (Prov. 3: 9, 10.) That sounds like a good plank in a platform of "farm relief." The Rich Fool had his barns filled with

plenty, but his heart was empty by refusing to honor God; preferring instead to take credit for his prosperity in a disastrous public utterance.

4. Man becomes a partner with God. "For we are laborers together with God." (1 Cor. 3: 9.) God puts into the fellowship of worker and God His power and love, and forgiveness and holiness, and goodness and truth. The infinite resources of the Infinite God are placed at the command of the man who will obey the great principles of stewardship in the matter of his handling money. On the other hand, a partnership with God asks that we put in all that we have, being willing to forsake everything in order that we may take up the Cross and follow Him. He does not always demand that we turn it all over to Him, usually preferring to keep it as a character-test and a means for building his kingdom on earth. But partnership is based on sharing. When a man takes God in as a partner in business, he earns, and saves, and spends, and gives, and accounts under the guidance of, and in the conscious presence of, his heavenly partner.

For the fine results that flow from the observance of such principles listen to this from Dr. Halford E. Luccock in "Studies in the Parables of Jesus": "Whenever a man who is a lover of money renounces his covetousness; when the lover of pleasure, or the man under the control of appetite, conquers the love of his habitual indulgence; when the proud man or woman casts pride aside and becomes humble; when the lazy man overcomes his love of 'slippered ease'; when the hard man becomes a little more human and sympathetic, then each is selling what he has and buying the Kingdom." Which is another way of saying that he has taken God in as his partner. "All things come of thee, and of thine own have we given thee. For we are strangers before thee, and sojourners, as all our fathers were; our days on earth are as a shadow." (1 Chron. 29: 15.) How long will it take us to learn that a man's life is not a part of his possessions?

THE SPIRITUAL IMPORTANCE OF MONEY

Jesus loves the successful man. He does not condemn the possession of wealth. He looked upon the rich and successful young ruler and he loved him. He was glad to welcome Zacchæus, a man of money. Jesus did not condemn the Rich Fool for having much goods. He condemned him for thinking he could feed his soul on "things." The same principle is at stake in the parable of Dives and Lazarus; in the "choked" channel in the Parable of the Sower; the Forgiven Debtor; the parables of the Pearl and the Hid Treasure; and in Jesus's statement about a rich man having a hard time getting into heaven. It is the love of money that is "the root of all evil" and not money itself.

The Bible refers to prayer about five hundred times, to faith less than five hundred times, and to material possessions more than one thousand times. Sixteen of Jesus's thirty-eight parables are clearly concerned with the stewardship of material possessions. Money is spiritual in function and in character. It can only be gotten as God gives the power for man to get it. It is the condensation of human wants and the embodiment of man's desires. It is significant that only beings who have souls can use it, exchange it, multiply it, and glorify it. Through it God speaks to man, thereby seeking to control him.

Money represents real cost in toil, sacrifice, saving, energy, effort, and character, so that it becomes a bit of coined character and a part of life and time and talents. Money may go out to save the world for Christ at home and abroad. Through silver and gold God joins himself to us. "What God hath joined together let not man put asunder." It is valueless in itself; but linked to God it may educate the underprivileged, establish libraries, clinics; or go into all the world to save souls.

The prostitution of money and the desecration of the dollar is the sin that catches millions. It was the stumblingblock upon which Israel fell; that caused the nations of Greece, and Rome, and Babylon to grasp for power and subsequently to fall. It has power to secure for the selfish soul his desire for luxury, ease, cars, houses, lands, diamonds, the pleasures of life and pampered idleness. It has power of life and death, of war and peace, of cursing and blessing.

Money is used to measure the cost of everything except life itself. But money is the most expensive thing in the world. We give life and head and hands and heart and health for it. We pay for it with time and abilities and

139

education and heritage. If we get it honestly, we put much prayer into the getting of it. Some buy their money at the cost of character and reputation and friendships and Christian opportunity. Money influences the courts of justice and sometimes blinds the man who holds the scales in his hands.

> "Through tattered clothes small vices do appear;
> Robes and furred gowns hide all. Plate sin with gold
> And the strong lance of justice hurtless breaks;
> Arm it in rags, a pigmy's straw does pierce it."
>
> ("King Lear," IV, vi, 168.)

Money may be a great aid to character and a great blessing to the Christian. It provides a wonderful outlet for his power, a way by which he may transmute silver and gold into achieved purposes. With it he may open the very doors of heaven and have blessings poured out upon him the like he cannot receive. He may take this stored-up energy, that represents his very self, and by sitting quietly in the pew of a church, drop some of it into the collection plate and shortly be serving God, through the gift, to the uttermost parts of the earth.

Since all money was first God's before it came into man's possession, the man who refuses to recognize God in the use and possession of money always taints his own soul. This is perhaps what we really mean when we talk about "tainted money"—it taints the man. It taints him with ingratitude, with selfishness, with covetousness, with dishonesty, and with the blood of his neighbors, dying without salvation by reason of his withholding his gifts to God.

Nathaniel Hawthorne in "Mosses from an Old Manse" has a story on "The Celestial Railroad"—a modern version of "Pilgrim's Progress." Among the more interesting of his descriptions is the one of Vanity Fair as seen on this Railroad trip. He recalls that occasionally members of Congress would recruit their pocketbooks by selling their constituents and how he was assured that in the city of Vanity and in Vanity Fair public officers have often sold their country at very moderate prices; that thousands were known to have sold their happiness for a whim, and gilded chains were purchased at great sacrifice. There were innumerable messes of pottage, piping hot, for such as chose to buy them with their birthrights, and many purchasers. Tracts of land and golden mansions in the Celestial City were often exchanged, at very disadvantageous rates, for a few years' lease on small, dismal, and inconvenient tenements. Hawthorne tells us that Prince Beelzebub himself took great interest in this sort of traffic and sometimes condescended to meddle with small matters. He was once seen bargaining with a miser for his soul. After much ingenious skirmishing on both sides, his highness succeeded in obtaining the miser's soul for about sixpence. With a smile, Beelzebub remarked that he was loser in the deal.

There are still those who sell out for gold, who prefer the Vanity Fair of the world that now is, to the eternal happiness of the world that is to be.

In God We Trust

From the records of the Treasury Department of the United States we learn that the first recognition of God on our national coins was contained in a letter from the Rev. M. R. Watkinson of Ridleyville, Pennsylvania, to the Secretary of the Treasury, Hon. S. P. Chase, under date of November 13, 1861. The letter reads: "One fact touching our currency has hitherto been seriously overlooked. I mean the recognition of Almighty God in some form on our coins. You are probably a Christian. What if our republic were now shattered beyond reconstruction? Would not the antiquaries of succeeding centuries rightly reason from our past that we were a heathen nation? What I propose is that, instead of the Goddess of Liberty, we shall have, next inside the thirteen stars, a ring inscribed with the words 'Perpetual Union'; within this ring the all-seeing eye crowned with a halo; beneath this eye the American flag, bearing in its field stars equal to the number of the States united; in the folds of the bars the words, 'God, liberty, law.' This would make a beautiful coin to which no citizen could object. This would relieve us from the ignominy of heathenism. This would place us openly under the Divine protection we have personally claimed. From my heart I have felt our national shame in disowning God as not the least of our national disasters."

Under date of November 20, 1861, Mr. Chase wrote as follows to the Director of the Mint, James Pollock, Esq.:

"No nation can be strong except in the strength of God, or safe except in His defense. The trust of our people in God should be declared on our national coins. Will you cause a device to be prepared without unnecessary delay with a motto expressing in the fewest and tersest words possible this national recognition?"

It was discovered that nothing could be done without legislation. In December, 1863, the Director of the Mint submitted to the Secretary of the Treasury for his approval designs for new one-, two-, and three-cent pieces on which it was proposed to use one of the following mottoes: "Our country: Our God" or "God, our trust." An act was passed April 22, 1864, changing the composition of the one-cent piece and authorizing the coinage of a two-cent piece, the devices to be fixed by the Director of the Mint, with the approval of the Secretary of the Treasury. It is upon the two-cent bronze piece that the motto, "In God We Trust," first appears, the motto being so worded after consultation between the two men to whom the matter was referred. By act of March 3, 1865, it was provided that in addition to the legend and device on the gold and silver coins of the United States, it should be lawful for the Director of the Mint, with the approval of the Secretary of the Treasury, to place the motto, "In God We Trust," on such coins as shall admit of the inscription thereon. Under this act the motto was placed on the double eagle, eagle, and half eagle, and also upon the dollar, half and quarter dollars, in the latter part of 1865. The coinage act of February 12, 1873, provided that the

Secretary of the Treasury may cause the motto, "In God We Trust," to be inscribed on such coins as shall admit of such motto.

The recital of this significant bit of history serves to remind us that a motto on national coinage does not always mean that it is written upon the hearts of our people. But surely our trust is in God. In him we trust for a leadership that shall put the spiritual emphasis first and keep us from going crazy over bursting barns and the goods of this life. In God we trust for a loyalty that shall build buildings, secure budgets, write programs, and execute Kingdom plans. In God we trust for liberality sufficient to send the story of Christ around the world. It is God's people, God's Church, God's program and budget and goals and standards. In God we trust and not in machinery. In God we trust for men, for motives, for methods, and for money with which to carry out His plan of world redemption. "Trust in the Lord with all thine heart; and lean not unto thine own understanding; in all thy way acknowledge him, and he shall direct thy paths" (Prov. 3: 5, 6.) The only way to overcome the insurmountable obstacle of unconverted attitude toward money and property, and to build the Kingdom of God, is to substitute a love for the trust in God. Dreams of youth are being drowned in business, mission endeavors are halted, and master iniquities are destroying our civilization because we have substituted trust in Gold for trust in God. The condition of our world should drive us to our knees in prayer and supplication before God, there to stay until we can get the power of the Holy Spirit and willingness of heart to "seek first the kingdom of God and his righteousness." Stewardship is a principle to be instilled rather than a method to be installed and mottoes have no meaning until they are written on the heart.

SOME MEN WHO EARLY LEARNED THIS

When William G. Duncan of Greenville, Kentucky, went to his eternal reward in 1929, one of his friends referred to him as a man who "could use this world without abusing it, and make friends with the mammon of unrighteousness in order to provide for a welcome in the Kingdom of God." Mr. Duncan, grown wealthy in this world's goods through handling coal and other products, was called by his Church "Not slothful in business, fervent in spirit, serving the Lord." He was an outstanding layman, officer in the Presbyterian Church and superintendent of his Sunday school. He was identified with three great enterprises—home missions, orphanage work, and education for the ministry. He had intended to be a minister, but his father's death caused him to change his plans. No one ever knew the real extent of his benevolences. He gave hundreds of thousands to the Kentucky Theological Seminary, orphanages, and mission enterprises. He early learned the art and joy of honest acquisition, and accepted his rapidly accumulating wealth as a stewardship. His money became a means of grace and he delighted to call God his "Divine Partner." Once when, with his board of directors gathered around him, he was

145

preparing to open a new mine, before putting the spade in the ground he halted the proceedings and dedicated the mine-that-was-to-be to God who had made it possible. He had put God first.

In a newspaper interview Fritz Kreisler is reported as saying: "I was born with music in my system. It was a gift of God. I did not acquire it. So I do not even deserve thanks for the music. Music is too sacred to be sold, and the outrageous prices charged by musical celebrities to-day are truly a crime against society. I never look upon the money I earn as my own. It is public money. It is only a fund intrusted to me for proper disbursement. I am constantly endeavoring to reduce my needs to the minimum. I feel morally guilty in ordering a costly meal, for it deprives some one else of a slice of bread, some child perhaps of a bottle of milk. My beloved wife feels exactly as I do about these things. In all these years of my so-called success in music we have not built a home for ourselves. Between it and us stand all the homeless in the world."

We are told that Emerson refused to accept an income of more than twelve hundred dollars a year, for he said he wanted to have time to think; that the early Christians refused to accept or retain money beyond their actual needs, for they preferred to have hearts at rest in order to soothe and sympathize. Hear money speak:

> "Dug from the mountainside or washed in the glen,
> Servant am I, or the master of men;
> Earn me, I bless you; steal me, I curse you;

THE CONQUEST OF COVETOUSNESS

Grasp me and hold me—a fiend shall possess you.
Lie for me; die for me; covet me; take me;
Angel or devil, I am just what you make me."

A short time ago the *Arkansas Methodist* carried this interesting statement by Dr. William Mayo, speaking for himself and his brother, Dr. Charles Mayo: "That holy money, as we call it, must go back into the service of that humanity which paid it to us. We try to take up the medical and surgical education of selected and promising men where the State leaves off. If we can train five hundred pairs of hands, we have helped hand on the torch; and we have hands to train now—nearly 300 of them, and a waiting list of 1,400. They are the ones that will carry on. From 1894 onward we have never used more than half of our incomes on ourselves and our families; latterly much less. My brother and I have both put ourselves on salaries. We live within them. The very roof of my house goes out of the possession of my family when I die. It is already turned over to the Foundation. I wouldn't want my children deprived of the fun and benefit of wanting something and going out to fight for it. And I think from the rich men with whom I have talked that this idea has penetrated far more deeply into American life than many imagine." Such an idea is the direct antithesis of the retirement plan that the Rich Fool had hit upon. And the fight is on in America between these two ideals of life. Charles Franklin Thwing, in "Education and Religion," a most helpful book, gives it as his opinion that while America is called a nation of sensualism and materialism, beneath the surface she is a nation of idealists; that at heart we believe in truth, in right, in the unseen, the unheard, the untouched, and the eternal, that pursuit of such principles and ideals makes it possible to accomplish the conquest of materialism and preserve our nation from the doom of the Rich Fool—the collapse of character and loss of soul.

> "Blessed with victory and peace,
>   May this heaven-rescued land
> Praise the Power that hath preserved
>   And made us a nation;
> Then conquer we must, when our
>   Cause it is just;
> And this be our motto:
>   'In God is our trust.'"

Henry W. Grady, according to his biographer, Joel Chandler Harris, as told in "The Life, Writings, and Speeches of Henry W. Grady," had hundreds of opportunities to write himself rich, but he never fell below the high and manly unselfishness that marked his career as a boy and a man. His dominant passion was the development of his beloved Southland, materially, spiritually, and culturally. He never sought or held public office, though repeatedly urged to do so. Had he served his own interests with half the zeal he served the interests of his people, he would have died a millionaire. His wealth during life and in death was in his love of sweet chairty, friendships, patriotism, patience, love, and fairness. Wherever he found suffering and sorrow or misery he became a partner to those in need until the need could be met. First he gave himself. In an editorial in the *Atlanta Constitution* on September 20, 1884, he said: "Never gamble. Of all the vices that enthrall men, this is the worst, the strongest, and most insidious. Outside of the morality of it, it is the poorest investment, the poorest business, the poorest fun. No man is safe who plays at all. It is easiest never to play. I never knew a gentleman and man of business who did not regret the time and money he wasted in it. A man who plays poker is unfit for every other business on earth."

TAKING GOD AS PARTNER

Every one is acquainted with the stories of John Huyler, the candy man; of A. A. Hyde, the mentholatum man; of Colgate, the soap man; of Nash, the Golden Rule clothing man; and of numerous other high-caliber business men who have opened accounts with their unseen but all powerful Partner, Jesus. Before the rewards of partnership can be reaped, the steps to partnership must be taken. Usually these steps are as follows:

1. We must put God first in our lives. Paul records with much joy, in writing to the Corinthians about the way the grace of God had been bestowed on the churches of Macedonia, which resulted in their eagerness to give money, that these people "first gave their own selves to the Lord, and unto us by the will of God" (2 Cor. 8: 5). To seek first the Kingdom means that we shall begin at the

beginning by giving our own selves. It is not our money that God would be partner to, but ourselves.

2. We must put God first in our money budgets. This means that we must make a budget and keep a budget. How shall we know that God is first, and that a just share of every dollar is going back into the service of God who gave it, if we have not been careful to set down the "income" and the "outgo." A good plan is to draw a diagram of a dollar, and begin with taking out at least one-tenth for God, then divide aright the rest of the dollars as follows: food, shelter, clothing, education, business, taxes, self-improvement, government, recreation, and so on. We are told that the average American spends his dollars as follows: Living expenses, 24½ cents; luxury, 22 cents; waste, 14 cents; miscellaneous, 13¼ cents; invests, 11 cents; crime, cure and care, 8½ cents; government, 4½ cents; schools, 1½ cents; religion, ¾ cent. That sounds like a budget that might have been compiled by the Rich Fool. It is apparent to the Christian that the places to cut in such a program are these: "Luxury," "Waste," and "Miscellaneous." Without disturbing your program for investment and education, and living and government support, or the prevention of and payment for crime, it is easily possible for us to get money enough to send the Gospel to the uttermost part of the earth by taking off some—not all—from the three above-mentioned items and adding to the cause of Christ and his Church.

3. It is necessary to remember that by putting God first in the budget, and by definitely setting aside a propor-

tionate part of the income to Him, beginning usually with one-tenth, we have not, nor can we, shut God out of full partnership in the nine-tenths that are left. We should put the cross of Christ at the center of the Dollar and every dollar, remembering the motto "In God we trust."

4. The fourth step in partnership is the establishment of the principle of stewardship in all phases of relationship to money. We must take God into partnership in the acquiring of money, which means that we will acquire it honestly; in saving money, which means that we will save it rightly; in spending money, which means that we will spend it wisely; in giving money, which means that we will give it freely; and in accounting for money, which means that we will account for it properly.

5. The fifth step in partnership concerns the establishment of definite principles of giving. The Bible teaches that we should give cheerfully (2 Cor. 9: 7), liberally (Luke 6: 38), sacrificially (2 Sam. 24: 24), humbly (Matt. 6: 3, 4), honorably (Prov. 3: 9), profitably (2 Cor. 9: 6), systematically (1 Cor. 16: 2), and proportionately (Deut. 16: 17). My giving must be with the proper motive, with the right incentive, and as an act of worship to Him who gave up the privilege of being rich in order that his poverty might make us rich.

Dr. O. N. Ritchie gives an interesting illustration of the principles and steps in budget-making in telling of how his friend Barney from Malita, in the Solomon Islands, put God in his budget. Barney went to Queensland to work on a sugar plantation, and there he met Jesus. When he returned home he was attacked by his heathen fellow men and forced to flee to New Zealand, where he was free to practice the principles of stewardship. He was brought to Christian Stewardship by reading the book of Malachi, and when he found that he had been robbing God he turned his heart and purse toward a new and a fuller life. One day the evangelist for the section of New Zealand in which Barney was now living heard a knock at his door. When he went out he found Barney holding a horse, saddled and bridled—his gift to the Lord to be used by the evangelist. Though but a young man getting started in business, Barney had taken the Lord in as his partner, giving each week two pounds to the Lord and living on eight shillings. Stewardship is a way to find life rather than a method to raise money.

REWARDS OF PARTNERSHIP

In his book, "Royal Partnership," Dr. M. E. Melvin devotes a chapter to "The Field of Partnership," presenting the facts that partnership with God is a creative partnership an accumulating partnership, an administering partnership, a participating partnership, and a rewarding partnership. It may be well for us to notice some of the rewards of partnership with God in this business of handling money and life.

First, it clarifies our motives. It places the emphasis upon the fact that "man's chief end is to glorify God and enjoy Him" rather than to glorify Gold and enjoy it. This partnership eliminates the feeling that we are driven to tasks, and substitutes the joy of working with God in accomplishing our life purposes. It is manifest that unless this generation can get hold of the ideal of property for the sake of personality, and begin to make it an instrument for better living instead of "high living," we need have little expectation of producing citizens of great spiritual power. Partnership with God clears up the purposes of life.

Second, partnership purifies our property interests. It puts God first, others second, and the property owner third in considering the use of property. Robert E. Lee once said: "He never loved who will quit anything of his religion to save his money." The Rich Fool when he was ready to retire, had he taken God into partnership in his plans, might have enjoyed the company of his own soul and the society of his fellow men. But he was forced to sit by and see his soul take its journey from a body that was now ready to return to the dust, forsaken, unpurified, lonely, and lost. His purposes were muddled by desire for Gold.

Third, partnership energizes our spiritual resources and harnesses them to the infinite purpose of God. It merges our limited resources with the infinite resources of God and together we carry out God's purpose on this earth. The intake of this partnership is through grace; the outlet is through life, time, money, and abilities. The great problem of the Church is how to transmute the things of this life into saved souls. God calls us to partnership with Him, aware that he has never addressed a call to a human soul that did not demand sacrifice, renunciation, and constant endeavor. But God always lives in calling distance of his partners.

Dr. W. M. MacKay in "The Men Whom Jesus Made" calls Judas "The man whom Jesus could not make." It is the tragic story of a fool who was not rich, yet who coveted and was lost. "Good were it for that man if he had never been born," said Jesus of him. He was avaricious to the extent of theft, and being a man of administrative gifts and treasurer of the band of Disciples, he attempted to serve God and mammon. This fool, too, had his soul required of him, "and he went to his own place." His story is the direct opposite of the rewards of partnership and we mention it to paint the contrast. Judas cut himself off from God, from his fellow men, and from very life itself. Alex Louis Fraser describes in "Life's Illusion" the man who cuts himself off from partnership with God:

"He toiled and saved his earnings every day,
  But starved his mind and grasped at common things;
His prisoned soul ne'er struggled out of clay,
  His better nature never found its wings.

He hoped to sit with happiness at last,
  Mansioned, sufficient, when he would be old;
But he was just a graveyard, and the past
  Left naught for him but a rude pile of gold."

After the similitude of Joel Chandler Harris with his "Uncle Remus" stories, Stoney and Shelby in "Black Genesis" have brought Brer Rabbit and his fellow creatures to us recently in the Gullah dialect. One of their best stories has to do with the Guinea Fowl and the Turtle. It seems that the Guinea Fowl was created, according to this folk-story, with a thick shell on his back, which not only was of great protection to him, but made it possible for him to forage for food in dangerous places that were not accessible or safe for the other creatures. The result was that the Guinea Fowl became fat and selfish and vain. Other creatures attempting to borrow his shell were repulsed. He refused to be a partner with his fellow creatures. But he became so fat that his shell begun to hurt him, to irritate him, so that when he would lie down to sleep the shell would keep him awake. One day he asked the Turtle, who up until that time had a tender back, to take care of his shell while he took a good rest. This the Turtle finally consented to do, with the result that when the Guinea Fowl took it off and placed it on the Turtle's back and lay down to sleep, the Turtle ran away with it never to return. It is not necessary to draw the moral, that many people become so absorbed in the desire for gain, and so wrapped up in themselves, that they lose the thing they value most.

John Wesley's Stewardship

It will be hard to find in all history the story of a man who rendered a better account of his stewardship of life and time and abilities and money than did John Wesley. He lived with the utmost economy and gave away the whole surplus of his income. When he got thirty pounds a year he lived on twenty-eight and gave away two; when he got sixty pounds he lived on twenty-eight and gave away thirty-two; when he later received ninety pounds, he lived on twenty-eight and gave away sixty-two; and later still, when he got one hundred and twenty pounds a year, he lived on twenty-eight and gave away ninety-two.

Wesley taught that the talent of money-making is not to be despised, but to be regarded as God-given and used for his glory. He emphasized in his life and teaching that money may be used to open the eyes of the blind, cause the lame to walk, and lift up the fallen on this earth. He said: "Gain all you can, save all you can, give all you can." "It is no more sinful to be rich than to be poor, but it is dangerous beyond expression; give something and you will be no poorer for it; grudge and fear not; lean upon the Lord and He will surely repay. If you earn but three shilling a week, give a penny of it, and you will never want. But I do not say this to you who have ten or fifteen shillings a week, and give only a penny. I have been ashamed for you, if you have not been ashamed for yourselves. Give in proportion to your substance. Open your eyes, your heart, your hand." Or again: "If you have a family, consider seriously before God how much each member of it wants in order to have what is needful for his life and godliness. This being done, fix your purpose to gain no more. As it comes daily or yearly, so let it go." Some one objects that he must provide for his children. "Certainly: but how?" asks Wesley. "By making them rich? Then you will probably make them heathen. Leave them enough to live on, not in idleness and luxury, but by honest industry. You will have no reward in heaven for what you lay up, but for what you lay out. Every pound you put in the earthly bank is sunk; it brings no interest above. But every pound you give to the poor, you put into the bank of heaven. And it will bring glorious interest.

It is said that a generous-hearted lady left Wesley a legacy of a thousand pounds. In a short time it was all given away. He wrote to his sister: "You do not consider that money never stays with me; it would burn me if it did. I throw it out of my hand as quickly as possible lest it should find a way to my heart; therefore you should have spoken to me in London before Miss Lewen's money flew away."

His last entry in his personal account book was made about six months before his death and reads: "For upwards of eighty-six years I have kept my accounts exactly. I will not attempt it any longer, being satisfied with the continual conviction that I save all I can, and give all I can, and that is all I have." Wesley was a great steward of his splendid intellect, of his time, and of his talents; and with reckless abandon he gave his life to his partner.

REASONS FOR PROPORTIONATE GIVING

Proportionate giving puts God first in the Christian's money budget and brings real happiness. By setting aside at least a tenth of the income for the cause of Christ, it is easy to systematize and budget the remainder of the income, which is also God's. It helps us to apportion the right amounts to food, shelter, clothing, education, and other things. Which means that proportionate giving, placing that first in the budget, elevates the whole matter of my relation to money.

Proportionate giving is a fundamental principle, having its origin in the mind and will of God. It is not "casual" but "causal" in the Christian's life. Every neglect of a principle retards Christian growth. This matter of proportionate giving is not a legalistic whip to drive money from the purse, but a great principle by which we may grow in grace.

Proportionate giving helps to avoid covetousness. Paul says, "The love of money is the root of all evil." He classes the sin of covetousness with the vilest of sins. But if we put God first in our money matters, it makes it easier to conduct business on the principle of sharing with others.

Proportionate giving develops loyalty to Christ and his program of world salvation. Budgets, and programs, and standards, and church machinery—these are secondary. The primary reason for a Christian's proportionate giving is internal need; in order to escape from things and put Christ and His Kingdom first. Having settled the problem by serving God with mammon, we seek for outlets for giving.

Proportionate giving releases the Christian's spiritual resources for Christ's use in Kingdom extension. Pentecost is always just around the corner. The coming of the Holy Spirit into our lives awaits our clearing the channel. Our minds and hands and hearts and spirits must be freed of unconsecrated money if our souls are to be free in the Master's service.

THE CONQUEST OF COVETOUSNESS

Proportionate giving releases money for the Kingdom. Production of money, in partnership with God, and, as part of God's plan, proportionate giving, elevate the daily occupation of the business man to a holy calling. This principle establishes Christian equality, before God, of all Church members. The plan of sharing is regular, systematic, proportionate, regardless of how irregular the income may be. God's promises are all conditional. We must meet the conditions to claim the promise.

Proportionate giving makes us partners with God in getting, saving, spending, giving, and accounting. By sharing the thing we are most tempted to covet we elevate all of life's affairs and make all things that we touch contribute to the telling of the Story of Christ, and thus we fulfill the real mission of the Christian. If we cannot put Christ first in our money matters, how can we put him first elseswhere?

Consider Jesus

Jesus is the best example of Christian Stewardship, and his life is the best answer to the foolishness of the Rich Fool of the parable. Jesus was a poor man. He was born in a stable and raised in poverty. He worked as a laboring man in a carpenter shop. When he began his ministry he had no organization to back him, no private income, and no temporal means of livelihood. He got no money for his preaching and wrought his miracles without remuneration. He went through his whole public ministry without a home. He said, "The foxes have holes, and the birds of the air have nests, but the Son of man hath nowhere to lay his head." As an itinerant preacher whose field was the world, he often slept out in the open, with the sky as his covering. He doubtless often went hungry. When he wanted to cross his favorite Galilee, he must borrow the boat; when he fed the multitudes, he must borrow the bread and the fish.

His support came largely from the gifts of women, but he never had any money of his own. His treasurer was a thief. Though he was the water of life, he often was thirsty, and though he was the bread of life, he often went without food. Thus he lived and toiled, and died, a poor man. The price that Judas got for Him was thirty pieces of silver—the price of a common slave. He ate the Last Supper in a borrowed room and went out to give his life up. He had not the price to hire another, and lonely, forsaken by his disciples, he carried his own Cross out to Golgotha. Having no money to leave, he commended his mother to John; he gave his garment to the soldiers to be gambled for, his peace to his disciples, his forgiveness to the thief on the cross, his heart and spirit to God who gave it, his life to the world. And he was buried in borrowed clothes in a borrowed tomb. "Thanks be unto God for his unspeakable gift." "For though he was rich, yet for our sakes he became poor, that we through his poverty might become rich."

There is the spring of all good stewardship.

V

STEWARDSHIP OF THE GOSPEL

PARABLE OF THE LABORERS IN THE VINEYARD

Matthew 20: 1-16

For the Realm of heaven is like a householder who went out early in the morning to hire laborers for his vineyard; and after agreeing with the laborers to pay them a shilling a day he sent them into his vineyard.

Then, on going out at nine o'clock he noticed some other laborers standing in the marketplace doing nothing; to them he said, "You go into the vineyard too, and I will give you whatever wage is fair." So they went in.

Going out again at twelve o'clock and at three o'clock, he did the same thing. And when he went out at five o'clock he came upon some others who were standing; he said to them, "Why have you stood doing nothing all the day?" "Because nobody hired us," they said. He told them, "You go into the vineyard too."

Now when evening came the master of the vineyard said to his bailiff, "Summon the laborers and pay them their wages, beginning with the last and going on to the first." When those who had been hired about five o'clock came, they got a shilling each. So when the first laborers came up, they supposed they would get more; but they too got each their shilling. And on getting it they grumbled at the householder. "These last," they said, "have only worked a single hour, and yet you have ranked them equal to us who have borne the brunt of the day's work and the heat." Then he replied to one of them, "My man, I am not wronging you. Did you not agree with me for a shilling? Take what belongs to you and be off. I chose to give this last man the same as you. Can I not do as I please with what belongs to me? Have you a grudge because I am generous?" So shall the last be first and the first last.   (Moffatt's Translation.)

STEWARDSHIP OF THE GOSPEL

> "He that of greatest works is finisher,
> Oft does them by the weakest minister;
> So Holy Writ in babes hath judgment shown,
> When judges have been babes; great floods have flown
> From simple sources; and great seas have dried,
> When miracles have by the greatest been denied."
> —*Shakespeare's "All's Well That Ends Well," II, i, 135.*

THE Parable of the Laborers in the Vineyard is the Master's answer to Peter's question, "What shall we get?" We go back into the nineteenth chapter of Matthew's Gospel to learn what prompted such a question. In verses 16-22 is the recorded story of a rich young man who, upon being invited to become a disciple, went away sorrowful, for he had great possessions and was unwilling to part with them in order to follow Jesus. He kept his wealth and lost his Saviour. He wanted eternal life, but he preferred earthly wealth. He wanted to be perfect, but wouldn't pay the price. And now listen to the Master: "And Jesus said to His disciples, 'I tell you truly, it is easier for a camel to get through a needle's eye than for a rich man to get into the Realm of God.' When the disciples heard this they were utterly astounded; they said, 'Who then can possibly be saved?'" Jesus looked at them and said, 'This is impossible for men, but anything is possible for God.' Then Peter replied, 'Well, we have left our all and followed you. Now what are we to get?' "

WHAT SHALL WE GET?

Peter's question was a perfectly natural one, and we are inclined to sympathize with him. True, it partakes of the natural, worldly man, but which one of us has not discovered himself asking a similar question about Christian work? With his infinite capacity for patience, Jesus gave Peter, and the others, a direct, immediate, hopeful, and satisfactory answer; that to those who had followed him there should be reserved twelve thrones and the joy of governing the twelve tribes, when He should finally come to His throne. And then he made them the matchless promise of a return of 10,000 per cent on any investment they might make: "Every one who has left brothers or sisters or father or mother or wife or children or lands or houses for my name's sake will get a hundred times as much and inherit life eternal." Figure it for yourself; if you put a dollar into the Kingdom, and get back a hundred dollars, isn't that one thousand per cent?

Not content with making two direct answers to Peter's question, Jesus, the matchless story-teller of all times, told the story of the laborers in the vineyard. This story therefore is best understood when it is connected with the narrative of the preceding chapter, and particularly with the question, "What are we to get?" Dr. Charles R. Erdman in his commentary, "The Gospel of Matthew," says of this parable: "It was simply designed to indicate the peril of refusing to enter the service of Christ and the danger of a commercial spirit in seeking for rewards in such service." Meaning, of course, temporal awards, for Jesus does promise definite rewards, as we have just seen, and does further indicate promised rewards in this parable. What, then, do we get?

The parable plainly tells us that if we enter the Saviour's service in the bargaining frame of mind, we get what we bargain for. And that brings us back to the principle of stewardship with which we began in the Parable of the Good Samaritan—namely, that the steward of Christ is a contributor first, rather than an acquirer, and that Christian happiness and success in life are based upon what we can give rather than what we can take out of life. When the lord of the vineyard went out early in the morning to hire laborers, there was evidently a spirit of acquisition in those he met, for "He bargained with them." Unwilling to trust his fairness and honesty to pay them a just wage at the close of the day, they drove a hard and fixed bargain. Regardless of the "collective bargain" plan in the business world, and any other arguments that might be deduced to prove that the earlier laborers were well within their rights to demand a fixed price, such "good business" is not so good when applied to Christian work, all of which is based upon the principle that it is better to give than to take, and all is voluntary.

In the great story of the Good Shepherd, Jesus has a name for the Christian worker who works exclusively for pay, whose eyes are on the wages, whose motive is gain, who counts profits, and perhaps drives close bargains. He says he is a "hireling." In a crisis, "when the wolf cometh" he flees, forgetting all about the sheep. What shall he get? He will get just what he bargains for—his shilling of worldly coin. But think of the poor sheep! Dr. Charles E. Jefferson, in "The Ministering Shepherd," calls our attention to the fact that while the world has many comforts and luxuries, it lacks love, and most of all needs shepherding. And Jesus is still primarily interested in individual persons. With the coming of steam engines, and factories and mills, and quick and amazing transportation, radio and television, the individual is about to be submerged by the mass in factories and buildings and groups and organizations. Men need a guide to get out of the maze of regimentation and impersonalization. God wants laborers in His vineyard of whom it may be said, as it was said of Barnabas, "He was a good man, and full of the Holy Ghost." There is to be seen at the foot of the Apennines a gravestone with this inscription in tribute to a mountain guide: "He was a good man and a good guide." That's the kind of laborers needed in the world that just now seems to be about to lose direction.

What shall we get? If we enter the Master's service in the spirit of contribution rather than of acquisition, we shall get inner happiness, power, and satisfaction. Jesus is our great example of the simple approach to inner power. He was constantly turning aside, while he worked on earth in his Father's vineyard, to get direction and help and comfort for loneliness. When the lord of the vineyard, as the story records, went out the second time, and the third and the fourth times, he found a people with no work to do, willing to take whatever wage their employer should see fit to pay. They were workers that delighted his heart and he promised to pay them whatever was right. They must have been happier in their work, for now they could work for the joy of working, and not just for the wage. He who works in such a spirit in our Master's vineyard will get plenty of power for his life, plenty of fellowship in service, plenty of unity with his brethren, plenty of courage for the task, plenty of protection from God, and plenty of eternal reward. The Christian who is more interested in dividing aright the word of God to people who are hungry for the bread of life than in the loaves and fishes of position or honor or satisfaction of personal ambition will always get a hundredfold more than he gives.

What shall we get? If we accept the invitation to become workers together with God, we shall receive great growth. We shall receive growth of the Kingdom by adding souls for our hire. We shall double our worth to the Saviour by adding another soul to His kingdom. We shall receive personal growth of capacity for enjoyment and usefulness. We shall receive growth in grace. We shall grow up toward God, out toward our fellow men, and inwardly in respect to our souls. We shall fit all the work we do, the troubles we meet, the thoughts we think, and the plans that we make into a growing life and be happy with our wage day by day. And we know that the life eternal, the gift of God, comes as the final pay-off.

How long will it take us to learn that not all of life can be put in a pay envelope? The things that cannot be put in a pay envelope are the rewards of Christian work in the vineyard of the Lord. How often have we seen the bargaining attitude in the church; people who possess money, and leisure, and social standing, and culture, who by reason of these think that they may dictate the policy of the church and come in for especial honor when they labor for the Lord. What we need most to emphasize is the fact that happiness comes largely through the the possession of the great intangible virtues which are the gift of God. We need to speed up our spiritual experiences if they are to keep pace with our prodigious physical, economic, and social growth. What shall we get? We shall get what we put in—plus God.

INVESTING WHERE YOU CAN'T LOSE

The gift of one man, who was anxious to put into life more than he might take out, shines out like a star in England to-day. And with the gift is a fine story. Robert Arthington of Leeds, a Cambridge graduate, lived in a single room, cooking his own meals; and he gave to Foreign Missions five million pounds on condition that it all be spent on pioneer work within twenty-five years. On a slip of paper, after his death, were found these words: "Gladly would I make the floor my bed, and a box my chair, and another box my table rather than that men

should perish for want of the knowledge of Christ."
When we remember that the parable of the vineyard is
preceded by the promise of a return of ten thousand per
cent on such an investment, it is interesting to speculate
on what Robert Arthington shall get. But one wonders
why and how wealthy Christians can overlook such gilt-
edged investments. Could it be true that Lowell is his-
torically accurate and prophetically correct when he says,
"When the Puritans made their fortunes, they lost their
religion"?

Miss Sue B. Haley, of Atlanta, Georgia, invested her
life in the home missions section of the vineyard. For
twenty-five years she toiled away in the South at winning
the lost in the homeland to Christ. Last year while ad-
dressing the young people of a great church, pleading
that they help with the great task of soul-winning, with
outstretched hands and with a smile of happiness, she
crumpled to the floor, and was not, for God took her.
She was a devoted steward of her life, time, abilities, and
possessions, she made an investment of her all, staking
her life against the promise of God. She trusted the
Master of the vineyard to take care of the wages. What
shall she get? A life of radiant happiness, example, and
loving-kindness here, and life eternal there.

It is not the amount that we put into the task, but the
fidelity of service, the trust, the attitude, the completeness
of surrender, and the diligence with which we labor that
counts in the end. All shall receive eternal life, regardless
of the time we enter the Master's service, but what of the

thousands who might be saved by our efforts if we enter early in the morning of life, enlisted fully in His service?

WHY SHALL WE WORK?

1. Because the Master of the vineyard says, "You go into the vineyard too." And shall we stand all the day idle when he tells us that the fields are white to the harvest and the laborers are few? The call, "Come unto me," is always followed by the command, "Go ye." All Christ ever asked for, we are told, in order to save the world, was "a cross on which to die." And he died for a lost world. "For God so loved the world, that he gave his only begotten Son, that whosoever believeth on him might not perish, but have everlasting life." When the Master says "Go" to us, He means that he is sharing his Cross, and its power to save, with us.

2. Because we are stewards of the message of the Gospel. It is a message of personal salvation, and the mission of the Church is the message of the Gospel to lost sinners. Christ was not primarily interested in reformation, in social salvation, in betterment of outward condition; he was interested first in the redemption of the individual. Over against the Pharisaic law of retaliation Jesus put the principle of love and forgiveness. Whereas the Church of his day condemned or condoned sin, Jesus came to bring the news that he could forgive the sinner. What a man! What a message! "I am not ashamed of the gospel of Christ; for it is the power of God unto salva-

tion, . . . to the Jew first, but also to the Greek." (Rom. 1:16.)

3. Because the world most needs, of all things, a message from God. It is required in Christians that they be people with a message. We may list as our possessions such things as personal charm, business ability, social standing, or intellectual superiority; but unless these are harnessed to the one motive of world salvation, they are valueless to Him who has called us into his vineyard. Speaking before a church court during his presidency, Woodrow Wilson said: "We who stand outside the active administration of the church, so to say, derive an illegitimate usury. We do not seem to add a great deal to its capital, but we do live on its investments." Over against that statement, put this immortal statement of Wilson, as quoted on the Tennessee War Memorial Building facade at Nashville, Tennessee: "America is privileged to give her blood and her might for the principles which gave her birth and happiness, and the position she has treasured." When we remember that Christ also loved the Church and gave his life for it; when we remember with what sacrifice the early fathers of the Church and our own forefathers have wrought out and handed over to us our Christian privileges; and when we remember that we are being called individually to seek the Kingdom first, and build on the foundation of the Apostles and Prophets and Fathers the enduring Kingdom of God, surely we will examine our motives of life and work and be found faithful in the labor of the Lord!

171

4. Because to win souls for Christ is the greatest work in the world. Henry Drummond once said, "The greatest thing in the world is love." True. And the greatest power in the world is the power of prayer; and the most valuable thing to a Christian is time; and the most dangerous thing in life is money; but the greatest work in the world is personal work to win souls. And this work is committed to us as a sacred stewardship. Christ's program is a challenging program; our churches have adequate machinery and plenty of money and plenty of people to accomplish that program. But we are short on motive and definite, personal enlistment.

5. Because a man's worth is as his motive is. The parable of the laborers in the vineyard would tell us that God's is not a time-clock, piece-measure, "stretched-out" plan of work, with victories and defeats entered on the credit and debit side of the Book of Life, because of the hour or conditions under which we began to work for Him. We may suffer handicaps of body or blood or environment; debility of will or thwarting of dreams through financial dependence of loved ones; we may enter the service at the last hour of the working day, and enter with an enfeebled personality; we may struggle on through life, suffering a thousand defeats while others leap to victory at the first attempt; but remember this: God judges us by the motives, and "while man looketh on the outward appearance, God looketh on the heart." Remember this too, that while Herod "stole along to his throne like a fox, ruled like a tiger, and died like a dog," Jesus, born at the end of his

reign, "came not to be ministered unto, but to minister and give his life a ransom for sin." With Jesus, the motive was the thing, and he never suffered a defeat. He stands out to-day, pleading for co-workers.

How Shall We Work?

The parable we are considering is clearly an exposition of the emphasis of the Master on the spirit as against the letter of the service, and an exposé of the hireling spirit in Christian work. Peter had drawn a proud contrast between the rich young ruler and the disciples of Jesus and asked a rather bad-spirited question. He got a wonderful promise and a merited reproof. In each case Jesus ended with the thought of the reversal in the position of the first and the last. The first to-day in noble offerings, great achievements, high honors; who serve for ostentation and in a spirit of pride, or in the hope of gain, thereby put themselves last in inner satisfaction and happiness; while those who give the cup of cold water, the two mites, the vase of ointment, in humility and sacrifice, have thereby and therewith purged their lives of dross and become first in inner joy and satisfaction. "The first shall be last, and the last first."

How shall we work? We shall work for the sheer joy of working. The man who does spiritual duties, takes office in the church, serves on committees and boards for the mere sake of the reward of place, position, power, and the commendation of men is letting the work revolve around him instead of Christ. He may be thoroughly secular in doing what he terms a "businesslike" job at a sacred task, and lose his real reward; while some hard-worked housekeeper, by doing a menial task from a Christian motive, has elevated a secular task to a sacred position. So with the banker, the lawyer, the doctor—by losing their lives they may find them again; while the full-time Christian worker by doing a purely mechanical service in a purely selfish way, by thus finding his life, may thus lose it.

How shall we work? With humble trust in the goodness of God and with charity toward our fellow workers. Surely that is the teaching of the parable. It is the story, among other things, of some grumblers. We have them in the church to-day. We have four kinds of workers— the tired, retired, tiresome, and tireless. Through the disciples to us comes a parable of warning against looking grudgingly at our fellow workers. We are taught that, however long-continued our work, abundant our labors, yet without charity to our brethren and humility, we lose out and become last. Pride and self-complacent estimation of our own work, like the fly in the ointment, will spoil our work, however great it may be, since the work can only permanently stand on trust and humility. To look down on, or despise, those who occupy a lower field of labor; to trust in quantity measurements, or time measurements; and to refuse to deny self and selfishness will rob us of our rewards.

How shall we work? As Jesus worked, not to do His own will, but the will of Him that sent Him. Kirby Page in "Jesus or Christianity" brings to us clearly the fact that blindness, legality, fear, self-centeredness, and indifference combined to bring about the death of Jesus. He shows, however, that Jesus had the alternative of saving his own life or becoming the Way of life. He chose to die. He lost Himself in devotion to His Father's will. Everywhere, in every church, community, trade, profession, industry, and calling, we come face to face with the fact that when a man loses himself in devotion to a great ideal, and works for the joy of working, he finds real life. Like Gideon of old, who went out one night to cut down the idols in the grove of Baal, and talked to God while he cut down the grove, so the tireless, happy worker in the vineyard of God gets the satisfaction of duty well done as he goes along. Listen to Whittier:

> "Thine to work as well as pray,
>   Clearing thorny wrongs away;
>   Plucking up the weeds of sin,
>   Letting heaven's warm sunshine in."

With What Instruments Shall We Work?

God has graciously provided us with tools by which we may accomplish the work in his vineyard. The first of these is a calling or vocation in life. The prevalent notion in some circles is that Jesus, in saying, "Render unto Cæsar the things that are Cæsar's, and unto God the things that are God's," made a separation between the sacred and the secular. He did not. He meant to let us know that all things are God's. He is the owner of life, time, talents, abilities, and money. He owns Cæsar and all that Cæsar is temporarily in possession of. Perhaps nothing has so hurt the Church as the futile attempt on the part of the Church member to draw a line between the sacred and the secular; between business and religion; between "full-time" and "part-time" service; and between Cæsar's and God's world. The man who ceases the attempt to divide his life into compartments, but who considers his vocation as a calling from God, has the best tool for fruitful labor for the Lord. He may bake bread, or bank, or farm, or manage, or preach, or teach, or write, or sing, or engage in any gainful occupation, and all the while, because he serves God through his vocation and in his vocation, he is occupied in a holy calling. Van Dyke[1] catches the spirit of the true workman in this verse:

"Every toiler in the quarry, every builder on the shore,
Every chopper in the palm-grove, every raftsman at the oar,

Hewing wood and drawing water, splitting stones and cleaving sod,
All the dusty ranks of labor, in the regiment of God,

March together toward His triumph, to the task His hands prepare:
Honest toil is holy service; faithful work is praise and prayer."

The second tool that God has given us is Time. He has given us a day in which to work—twenty-four hours, no more or less to anyone. It is time enough to do the work God has handed to us to do. Time can be abused, wasted, idled away, or slept away; or it may be redeemed, conserved, budgeted, used wisely for self-

---

[1] From "Collected Poems." Used by permission of Scribner's.

improvement, growth in grace, and the service and salvation of others. It is the most valuable thing that a Christian has. We have devoted much space in a previous chapter to this subject in discussing the parable of the ten virgins.

The third tool is the home in which we live. Through the dedication of the home to God, the practice of family prayer, the development of family ties, and the consecration of family opportunities, the home may be made to minister to the school, the church, the state, and the building of the Kingdom of God. Over the threshold of the home enter many who might be saved if the home could be used as a means to that end. It should be remembered that the home belongs to God, is given to man, and is to be occupied and used as a stewardship— a means to an end. The family altar alters the home, ennobles the home, enriches the lives of those in the home, and becomes a mighty instrument for salvation through the home. In "The Changing Family," G. W. Fiske has shown with what monster difficulties the modern home must contend, what contrary currents are blowing against it, and what elements in modern life tend to disintegrate it. But he agrees that we must strengthen, maintain, reënforce, and rebuild this fundamental institution, the hope of the State, the Church, the Kingdom. And in this great work the housekeeper is the chief home-maker. It "takes a heap o' living in a house to make it home," and it takes a heap of loving and praying and working to make a Christian home. But it is surely worth the price.

The fourth tool is money. It is the most interesting thing and the most dangerous thing a Christian has. All of us have some of it, and all of us want some more of it. Elsewhere we have discussed the spiritual significance of it, the power of it, and the curse of it. It must be remembered that, when used as a tool for the Kingdom, it blesses the giver and the object to which it is given. We have all found, when we try to catch it, keep it, and hoard it, that it has a detrimental effect on our minds, our wills, and our souls. We have always found that when we release it for the service and salvation of others it returns and crowns us with satisfaction and happiness and Christian success. God owns the earth, the mine, the bullion, the refinery, the assay plant, the bank, the bonds, the buildings, and the fields and barns. We owe it all to God. The Christian not only has money to give, but he has a collection plate to put it in—a mighty tool by which he may sit in the pew of his church and reach out to the uttermost part of the earth. Into the collection plate he may put regularly, systematically, and proportionately a bit of himself transmuted into money and surcharged with divine power as it goes on its way of service and salvation. The divine plan is 1 Corinthians 16: 2.

The fifth tool is the Gospel. When the Master of the world-vineyard said, "Go ye," he put a mighty instrument into the hands of every one who obeyed or shall obey. He put the story of a virgin birth, a sinless life, a triumphant ministry, a death on the Cross, burial in a borrowed tomb, a glorious resurrection, and a promise that He would come again. What a Gospel! It is the hope of the world. Our stewardship of that Gospel includes work, worship, witnessing, and giving. These are the four essential things that constitute faithfulness in the carrying of the Gospel. Shall we ever forget that the Gospel is a story? It is not first of all a series of books within a Book—it is the story of a life that was lived, of a death, of a crucifixion, and of a resurrection. That story is the mightiest tool that a Christian can use on the face of this earth. It can be told through life's endowments, natural abilities, physical strength; through preaching, teaching, and healing; through influence, fortune, or life-calling. It can be told! It is a trust—a stewardship.

In recounting the story of the rise and growth of the influence of the Stewardship movement in recent years, Dr. John M. Versteeg in "Perpetuating Pentecost" shows that one fault with the movement in its early days was that the "managers got the better of the messengers" and manipulated the movement in the interest of the ecclesiastical boards, thus making what God designed as a means to an end, an end in itself. Leaders everywhere are becoming aware, however, that stewardship is something God does for man, changing his motives, empowering him, and substituting dynamics for mechanics in his life and in the life of his Church. It is being taken out of the hands of the promoters and given to the prophets; out of the hands of the managers and given to the messengers. We are stewards of the Gospel.

Where Shall We Work?

We shall work where the need is greatest. Jesus was concerned for the multitude who were as sheep having no shepherd. He is concerned to-day, as we should be concerned most, with the lost, the last, and the least. Regardless of race, or creed, or color, or border, or breed, or birth, we should labor in that part of the vineyard where the need is greatest. It may be among the tens of thousands of foreigners in our midst, or among the noble but neglected people of the mountains, or with the Indian, or with the negroes, or with the great industrial peoples. Anyone is underprivileged who has not heard the story of the Gospel to the salvation of his or her soul. We may find the unsaved at our own door, in our own city, and even within the assembled congregations in our own churches.

Much labor of leadership must be exercised within our Church membership. It is said that at least seventy per cent of the more than 24,000,000 Church members in the United States are unenlisted in the Gospel work. We must enlist their lives first, and then their assets of time, money, and opportunities. These unenlisted people in our churches constitute the real gold mine of undiscovered development in the Kingdom of God. From this group could come sufficient power to win the whole world to Christ in this generation if they could be called to work in the vineyard of the Master. The Master's question, "Why have ye stood here all the day idle?" may peculiarly apply to them. But remember the answer of the workers in the parable, that "no man hath hired us." And there are a host of people who need instruction in how to work and where to work. Let them not say that they are idle because the leaders have not put them at the tasks they are best fitted to perform.

Where shall we work? In fields, white to the harvest, that stretch out to the uttermost part of the earth—Africa, South America, China, Japan, Europe, and to the ends of the earth. God is still calling to young men and women to go out and take up the task where the martyrs left off; to preach, and teach, and heal under conditions that are outwardly altogether changed from that of the former days, but among people whose basic need is ever the same—salvation from sin. God did not quit working when Livingstone fell asleep, when Dan Crawford laid down his tools, when Judson finished his appointed course, when Borden of Yale died on his way to India, or when the heralds of the Cross were slain in the Boxer rebellion. God did not quit when the business depressions of former days made the financial going hard, or when the drought of more recent times made the future look dark. God has not quit because of a revolution in the Orient or in South America. God has not quit working, or witnessing, or speaking to men. He is still working his purpose out, and He works where the need is. God has not quit. Shall we quit?

Where shall we work? Let us work among the working people of the world. For illustration, let us work among the cotton mill people of the South, where just now the going is pretty hard. The cotton mill operative is caught between the upper millstone of this machine-made and machine-mad civilization, with its demand for uniformity, conformity, and mass production and the nether millstone of high-pressure salesmanship and glittering appeals to luxury and comfort. The worker becomes a "hand" or a number. Because the going is still harder on the farm, by reason of drought and bad years, he is forced to take a very low wage for his work. We rejoice in the movement, instituted by the National Textile Institute, that will eventually eliminate all night work. But what will it advantage if the mills do away with night work, and cut the women and children out of drudgery, if there is no increase in the pay for those who remain at work? There is need for the application of the Gospel to both employer and employee—that the latter may give an honest day's work and that the former may give an honest wage. What shall it profit the capitalist if he gain the demanded dividends for those who sit around the director's table if he crush the life and soul out of the worker and lose his own soul while saving his life and the mansion on the hill? It will be fine if we can capture the centers of culture at the universities and educational institutions and elsewhere; but what if in the meantime we neglect the masses of industrial workers who form the very base of all permanent progress? If we are looking for a place to make great investments in the interest of the Gospel of Christ, the Church may find here her greatest opportunity and her most neglected field.

THE VINEYARD IS THE WORLD

Two good books setting forth the mission task of the Church, recently come from the press, are "Near Neighbors," by Dr. Homer McMillan, and "The Field Is the World," by Dr. James I. Vance. The former has to do with the task in America, while the latter deals with the larger view of the task as it applies to the mission fields abroad. But notice how the two authors agree in stating the scope of the work and the field to be occupied. Dr. McMillan begins his book by saying, "Every problem in the nation's life is essentially a missionary problem," and closes his book with this statement: "The Gospel is the only power the world has ever known that can bring all races and people into harmony with God and peace with one another." Dr. Vance states at the beginning of his book, "Christ's task was to bring a lost world back to God, to rebuild society, to establish a civilization of good will, to found the brotherhood," and closes with this: "There will be no return of Pentecost, on any centennial anniversary, to a church that is devoid of missionary zeal. If we are to have a great revival, it must have room to spread, and a corner is not big enough. The field is the world, and God is sounding out his ancient order: 'Speak to the children of Israel, that they go forward.'" Dr. Vance believes that the missionary challenge is threefold: the challenge of the Church to a world that is bankrupt and shot to pieces by sin, hate, and fear; the challenge of Christianity to the warring races; and the challenge of Christ to all other religious leaders and teachers and founders and faiths. But he believes, as do we all, that a Church consecrated to Christ can build a new world.

To build this new world, the Church must become the voice of one crying in the present wilderness of confusion, perplexity, despair, mass production, unemployment, and paralysis of high vision and deep motive through fear. The ministers and other leaders of the churches must be released from serving tables and being good organization executives, to become again the prophets for such a time as this. The way of the Lord must be prepared anew, by the herald who, with all the passion of a soul unafraid, points again to the Lamb of God which taketh away the sin of the world.

Roy Dickinson, in a recent issue of *Printer's Ink Monthy,* writes interestingly and effectively on the best way to get out of the business doldrums. He says: "The times have been such that every trouble from a bad breakfast to a bad drought invites a new invasion of personal gloom. So many people have been submerged in an ocean of apprehension, that some of them now believe the world is going on the rocks." Mr. Dickinson shows that the battle against despair, and fear, and poverty, and unemployment has been going on for centuries; but that temporary setbacks have always served as jumping off places for men of vision; and that in spite of the defeatists, prophets of despair, and gloomy philosophers who want the world to slide backward, we shall be led out of the doldrums by the men of vision of the present age, by men who bring into the troubled world ideas, courage, and resourcefulness. He asks the question, "When do we sail out of the doldrums?" and answers: "The day every man pulls hard on his oar." What a sermon from a business man to church leaders! In the midst of a spiritual calm, surrounded by the contrary winds of a bewildered world, the Church has her sailing orders, and knows her compass directions for sailing out of the doldrums. "I am the Way," says the master of the Vineyard, the ruler of wind and wave. We do not have to wait for favorable winds, for we are in a power-driven ship. We need only that we shall wait until we receive the power, for all the ship's machinery is of no avail unless and until it is empowered by the "dynamite" of God. And while the figure is a little mixed, we then need to apply to the Church's tasks the business principle of Mr. Dickinson for the cure of the depressions—we need every man to pull hard on his own oar, in Church-wide coöperation.

Work that counts for conquest in the world vineyard calls for the sacrificial giving of life. In the twenty-first chapter of Matthew Jesus gives three great parables—the parable of the lost son, showing his concern for the lost; the parable of the wicked husbandman, showing how the Son of God gives his life, and the rejection of the cornerstone by the builders; and the parable of the marriage feast and the great invitation. The three constitute the plan of salvation, though any one has its lesson and may be studied alone. But it took the life of the Son, as he searched for the lost, to prove his right to issue the invitation to come to the feast. And it takes life to-day to prove love.

The Associated Press sent out over their service wires, in connection with the opening of the London Naval Conference in January, 1930, one of those matchless human interest stories that sometimes "break" through staid news of regular headlines. This story concerned a young man with a heroic sense of duty. Just a few moments before the speech of King George, opening the Conference, was to go on the air for world-wide broadcasting, Mr. Walter Vivian, on duty at the Columbia Broadcasting Station at New York's receiving and rebroadcasting studio, discovered that something was the matter with the wiring. He knew that it would take at least twenty minutes to make the necessary repairs, and that in the meantime the waiting thousands would miss the King of England's message. Without hesitation he grasped the ends of the broken wires, wires that were broken by some one's carelessness, and with one in each hand he restored the broken circuit. The shock of the two hundred and fifty volt charge and the leakage of the current shook his arms violently and burned his hands, but he held on at the peril of his life while the King's message went through—the King's message on peace.

It costs life to carry the message of the King of Kings to a world that is lost in sin. Dr. Nicholas Murray Butler, who has delivered effective lectures on permanent peace in all parts of the world, has recently collected these lectures into one volume called "The Path to Peace." His steps on the path to peace are: first, the ethnic unity of a nation; second, geographic unity; third, economic unity; and fourth, independence. After that comes the international mind and world peace. Dr. Butler's suggestion for peace as it applies particularly to the United States is that she should join France in renunciation of war as a policy, agree upon a definition of what constitutes an aggressor nation, and then agree not to permit the giving of aid and comfort to aggressor nations. Which means that, if we are to have permanent peace, we must bring the millions of individual persons who compose the nations to want peace. Which means that there must be much giving up, giving in, and giving over to; that there must be much giving of life in heroic consecration to the Prince of Peace before his message of peace can be brought to the war-scarred and war-scared world. It is the same route of faith that the heroes of the Hebrew hall of fame trod—Abraham, Isaac, Jacob, Joseph, Moses, Rahab, Miriam, Esther, Ruth, Elijah, Zachariah, and others who gambled their lives on their faith in the ultimate triumph of righteousness and died in faith, not having yet received the promise.

Jesus, the Steward

The vineyard is the world, and Jesus is the best example we have of how to be a good steward of the vineyard. He recognized his accountability to God; was always about his Father's business, had a deep sense of his great mission in life; had a heroic attitude toward the proper use of his time, abilities, and powers of personality; he turned his back on things that meant comfort, acquisition, aggrandizement, fame, and position; and finally gave his life to make redemption available for all men. Jesus did much preaching and teaching and healing and miracle-working, but all that he did was a means to one great end and stewardship—to do his Father's will as declared in John 3:16. His way to accomplishment was the way of the Cross. Temptations came for him to turn aside and become unfaithful (Matt. 4:1-11), but he remained faithful to his stewardship (Heb. 3:1, 2), careful in his use of time (John 9:1-4), effective in his use of power (John 6:1-14), compassionate in love for others (John 11:35), and turning his face toward God cried, "It is finished"—a perfect life, a sacrificial death, a glorious stewardship (John 19:30).

The world has plenty of bidders for the life, the purse, the abilities, and the companionship and fellowship of her people, but God's Son, alone, is bidding in terms of the statement, "My son, give me thine heart." Henry W. Grady once wrote: "If creeds are put at peace and every man who wears the Christian armor will go forth to plead the cause of the meek and lowly Nazarene, whose love steals into the heart of man as balm of flowers into the pulses of the summer evening—then we shall see the hosts of doubt and skepticism put to rout." Of Mr. Grady, who himself illustrated in his own life the theme of that statement, the great preacher, DeWitt Talmage, said:

"Mr. Grady not only demonstrated that an editor may be a Christian, but that a very great intellect may be Gospelized." In the same public address, in which this tribute was paid to Mr. Grady, Dr. Talmage referred to an interview he had just had with William E. Gladstone, in which the great Gladstone said: "Sir, talk about the questions of the day! There is but one question, and that is the Gospel. That can, and will, correct everything." Dr. L. P. Jacks, who has helped us with many good books from his pen, and stimulated Christian thinking and action greatly, makes us see that the Gospel is really a story of a life that was lived. That's just what we need to see. We need to know that something really worth talking about took place back there in Palestine, making it possible for us to have a story to tell. We must live such a life as to tell out that story. And we must begin at Calvary.

Why Stand All the Day Idle?

The laborers in the vineyard had a good excuse for being idle—no man had given them anything to do. What excuse have we, now that we know what the work is, where it is, what tools we have to work with, and what motive should impel us? Is the task of the vineyard so large as to be vague in our minds? Then, suppose we begin by the intensive cultivation of one section of the Lord's vineyard. Shall we take a concrete case of need? Then listen to the report made recently, as a result of a survey of conditions among the negroes of Richmond, Virginia, a great cultural, educational, and industrial center: "The negro death rate is 20.43 per thousand as against that of the whites, 11.54. In infant mortality, tuberculosis, blindness, and in every adverse social situation, negro rates far outstrip the white. Only a few are making a living wage; they live in crowded, insanitary homes. Almost everything seems to be wrong with the houses: leaking roofs, plastering down, paper, painting, or kalsomining needed everywhere, porches, fences, gutters broken, plumbing defects of every kind." One-third of the families investigated had no water in the kitchen; three-fourths had no bathtubs; three-fourths had only outside toilets. The streets are dirty, bad, muddy and unpaved, dark; while rents are higher than for the corresponding grade for white people. Many of the negroes have no knowledge of how to take care of money, how to buy or keep house. Most of the mothers work outside the home, and yet have no protection for their children while they work. All these things are revealed in a survey that says, "In Richmond, as elsewhere, the negro's opportunities for wholesome recreation are almost non-existent." About half as much per capita is spent on their education as is spent on the education of the white children. And the education they get does not fit them for employment in the lines of employment for which they are eligible. If you think that such conditions are peculiar to Richmond, lay the measuring rod by conditions in Chicago, Detroit, New York, or any other city. If you think that such conditions are peculiar to the negro, make a careful survey of the foreign settlements; or of the marginal communities in your midst. Why do we stand all the day idle when we know there are such pressing needs to lift and love and save? There is nothing so complex as the "simple Gospel." The principles of Jesus must be applied not only to the individual life, but through the individual life to all social and economic conditions. We cannot have universal peace or world brotherhood until the principles of Jesus and the spirit of his stewardship pervade our thinking and our actions.

STEWARDSHIP OF WORK

When the angels of the Lord appeared to the shepherds, to herald the announcement of the birth of Jesus in the manger, the Book tells us that they were busy watching their sheep. Most of us are inclined to believe that visions come to us only in solitude, while we are meditating or reading God's word, or perhaps engaged in distinctive Christian work. But if we read over the list of the successful and happy we will find that most visions really come out of the midst of a busy day at the office, in the home, at daily labor, and in the fields of active labor. It may be at the desk or loom, the roaring market place, the store, the pulpit, the kitchen, or in the hurried routine of social activity. God does not want us after we have finished our day's work if he cannot have us while we are at the job. He wants us to serve him in and through the daily grind. If I am ashamed of the work I am in, then I may be sure that Jesus is also ashamed of me.

Poverty of earthly income in money is not necessary be-

191

fore we have vision of the world needs. It is true that Luther was born among the mines, Columbus in poverty at Genoa; that Lincoln was born in a cabin; Livingstone was born in a humble home; and so was Hogarth, and Haydn—and on and on we might go with an inexhaustible list of leaders. But it is not in birth, or nationality, or learning that vision, and happiness, and success come. They come from the contribution that one makes through his daily walk, work, witness, and conversation, to the betterment of the world, to the coming of the Prince of Peace, to the salvation of the lost. "I will consider my work as a vocation to which I am called of God to serve the highest interests both of myself and my fellow men," reads an item from the platform of a Christian steward. My service for the perfect Steward, Jesus, is not by compulsion from without, but by impulsion from within.

Canon Donaldson has given a list of what he calls the seven deadly sins of to-day. They are: (1) Policies without principles—the win-at-any-price idea; (2) Wealth without work—something we are all looking for; (3) Pleasure without conscience—I am not my brother's keeper; (4) Knowledge without character—accomplished crooks; (5) Business without morality—every man for himself, and so on; (6) Science without humanity— modern instruments of war; (7) Worship without sacrifice—mere lip service. We may well add another: Church membership without vision of a redeemed world and a passion for souls—marking time, and waiting to die.

Perhaps the one great question that still remains unanswered is, "Why stand ye all the day idle?" or, as Moffatt puts it, "Why have you stood doing nothing all day?" We cannot answer as did the laborers of the parable. We have the command of the Master of the vineyard, we have the instruments with which to work, the Lord is calling for laborers, the harvest is ready, and we are called to go work.

> "Up, and be doing! The time is brief,
> And life is frail as the autumn leaf.
> The day is bright and the sun is high,
> Erelong it will fade from the glowing sky;
> And the harvest is ripe and the fields are wide,
> And thou, at thine ease, mayest not abide.
> The reapers are few and far between,
> And death is abroad with his sickle keen.
> Go forth and labor! A crown awaits
> The faithful servant at heaven's gates;
> Work with thy might ere the day of grace
> Is spent, ere the night steals on apace.
> The Master has given his pledge divine,
> 'Who winneth souls like the stars shall shine.'"
> —*Anonymous*.

In "Evangelism, a Graphic Survey," Herman C. Weber shows the place of stewardship in the Church's complete program in the following outline: (1) Prayer—the Church talks with God; (2) Education—the Church learns from God; (3) Stewardship—the Church decides for God; (4) Evangelism—the Church works for God; (5) Service—the Church works like God. This places stewardship in the heart of the Church's plans for Kingdom work. He sets forth the fact that stewardship is the very atmosphere of decision, the entrance of God into all choices, and giving Him complete right of way in life.

God has given to the Church a task never committed solely to any other organization—the task and joy of presenting the Person and telling the Story of Jesus to all men everywhere. Evangelism brings the riches and resources of Christ to man; Stewardship brings the riches and resources of man to Christ and makes them available for world salvation. The Church has many ways of doing this, but only one Way to present; many plans conceived of men, but only one Power to accomplish her plans; many budgets to finance her work, but one Bible-plan of salvation; many programs, but one Person; many goals, but one God; various standards, but one Saviour; much organization, but one ordained task; much machinery, but one mission. "Let a man so account of us, as of the ministers of Christ, and stewards of the mysteries of God. Moreover it is required in stewards, that a man be found faithful." (1 Cor. 4: 1, 2.) "Who then is that faithful and wise steward, whom his lord shall make ruler over his household, to give them their portion of meat in due season?" (Luke 12: 42.) We are stewards of the Gospel. We are to be dispensers as well as depositories of the Gospel. God promises happiness and reward to the steward who is faithful over the assignment to which he has been assigned: "Blessed is that servant, whom his lord when he cometh shall find so doing. Of a turth I say unto you, that he will make him ruler over all that he hath." (Luke 12: 43, 44.)

VI

THE CONQUERING LIFE

BUILDING A TOWER AND WAGING WARFARE

Luke 14: 25-35

"THERE were large crowds traveling with him; so he turned and said to them,

"If anyone comes to me and does not hate his father and mother and
    wife and children and brothers and sisters, aye and his own life,
  He cannot be a disciple of mine;
Whoever does not carry his own cross and come after me,
  He cannot be a disciple of mine.

For which of you wants to build a tower and does not first sit down to calculate the expense, to see if he has enough money to complete it?—in case, after he has laid the foundation and is unable to finish the building, all the spectators start to make fun of him, saying, 'This fellow started to build but he could not finish it.' Or what king sets out to fight against another king without first setting down to deliberate whether with ten thousand men he can encounter the king who is attacking him with twenty thousand? If he cannot, when the other king is still at a distance he will send an embasy to do homage to him.

"So with everyone of you who will not part with all of his goods—
  He cannot be a disciple of mine.

"Salt is excellent indeed: but if salt becomes insipid, what will restore its flavor? It is no use for either soil or dunghill, it is flung out. He who has an ear, let him listen to this."

(Moffatt's Translation.)

THE CONQUERING LIFE

"The web of our life is of a mingled yarn, good
And ill together; our virtues would be proud, if
Our faults whipped them not; and our lives would
Despair, if they were not cherished by our virtues."
—*Shakespeare's "All's Well That Ends Well," IV, iii, 82.*

"There's a divinity that shapes our ends,
Rough-hew them how we will."
—*Shakespeare's "Hamlet."*

JESUS, in his life and death, is the undeniable example of the Conquering Life as illustrated in the parable of the building of the tower and the king going to war. With his growing popularity, knowing that temporal power and conquest were just around the corner for him, if he would have it, he counted the cost. He was God's gift to the world for the purpose of redemption. His life and the affairs of his life were a trusteeship with that one purpose in view. His way to conquest was by way of the Cross. He "endured the cross, despising the shame," for he had counted the cost of conquest. The Person of the matchless Story-Teller is the best proof of the truth of the parable, and the best incentive to live the conquering life of Christian Stewardship. At the time of the story Pilate had started, but was unable to complete, because of lack of funds, a magnificently projected aqueduct. It was not unusual, we are told, for people of that day to initiate plans and begin to erect great public buildings that could not be completed. As was the case then, so now, uncompleted buildings, extinguished enthusiasm, and cooled ardor for life's conquests are in the same class. Jesus would ask then, as now, Can you build your life on the plan of the Sermon on the Mount? Can go through to the end? The parable of the wicked husbandman tells the story of the giving of life when the son of the owner of the vineyard is slain by the tenant; the parables of the lost sheep and the lost son tell stories illustrating the reclamation of life and rejoicing therefor. The parable of the tower and going to war tells us the supreme importance of counting the cost of life if we would conquer as Christians. It was a time of reckless warfare as well as of thoughtless building. It was about this time that Herod, after divorcing his wife, the daughter of Aretas, was ingloriously defeated in battle by Aretas. Herod's whole life illustrates the fact of defeat and ignominious death through failure to pitch life on a high plane and count the cost.

THE ODDS ARE AGAINST US

When Jesus, in the parable, stated the odds of two to one, he was challenging to the heroic in life. He is asking that life's choices be made, and life be planned with the understanding that we "seek first the kingdom of God, and his righteousness." As he clearly states, not even a man's family or closest friends shall deter him from following Christ. There is a clash of claims to-day. A machine-made civilization, with its ability to deliver the goods of luxury and comfort, bids us live the nonchalant, lazy, drifting, and easy life—the life that sues for peace at any price rather than marshal the sterner forces and fight to the finish. Such a life ends in the haunted house of the coward's compromise. Jesus bids us live the life of self-denial, of stern self-discipline, of hard work, and continual fighting with the forces of evil. But he promises us that such a life, shot through with a regal passion, shall not only conquer here but live in a "mansion not made with hands" hereafter. When the rich, young ruler was challenged with Jesus's demand that he sell all he had, give it to the poor, and come follow him, he decided in favor of the luggage of life. There follow in his train to-day a horde of spineless, selfish, nerveless individuals who either refuse or neglect the Christian way of life because they are absorbed in the "things" that a purely secular existence can give. There can be little doubt of the tremendous pull to-day of the teachings of Humanism. It preaches a trust in human ingenuity, a reliance on man's inventive genius, and his ability to find in the world around him help in the time of need. But the physical freedom of a strong body, the mental pride in a trained mind, indicate that back of them there is constructive exercise, there is a channelizing of the mind. Jesus would have us sit at the training table for the soul. The highest type of heroism is not the courage and nerve of the warrior, facing the foe, but the moral courage to face the daily issues of life, opposing the wrong and upholding the right.

A Sheik Who Won Out

The story of Abraham is the story of a sheik who, with odds against him, became a steward of life and a trustee of the promise of God. God was looking for a man to become the head of his chosen people. Abraham's age, his business success, and his heritage were all against him. But at seventy-five years of age, when God asked him to count the cost of leaving his native land, his home, his people, and his business, "by faith Abraham, when he was called to go out to a place which he should receive for an inheritance, obeyed; and went out not knowing whither he went; . . . for he looked for a city which hath foundations, whose maker and builder is God." He became the progenitor of the Hebrews, the father of the faithful, friend of God. God owned this man's life. In his occupancy of the land, in his selection of a wife, in offering up Isaac, he always asked the will of God. He became a prince among neighboring chieftains, and when he died, at 175 years of age, he was a rich man in flocks and herds, and silver and gold. He had lived one hundred glorious years as a steward of his life since the day that God called him, and he had answered after counting the cost. Although he was called upon to forsake his gods— the gods of the sun and moon and the five planets that were visible, he gladly did so under the compulsion of his great faith in God as the creator, preserver, and owner of the earth and all the people therein. We live to-day in a promissory world, just as Abraham did. We are strangers and pilgrims here in a land of unfulfilled dreams and unrealized ideals, of undeveloped ambitions, unrivaled opportunities, and unequaled challenges to noble living. But God stands outside the door of this new day in which we live, and knocks, as he did in the day of Abraham. He too has his promises, just as the life around us has its promises of material success. Through friendships, and family, and church, and school God is calling us to the life of conquest. Over against the life that Abraham lived we have the story of Lot, who pitched his tent toward Sodom—toward wealth and social position, and luxury and comfort, and the good things of this life. Although Abraham was able to rescue Lot from the hands of the four kings that once captured him, the time finally came when, with the destruction of his home town by fire, Lot barely escaped with his life. Some one has said that to Abraham God's promises were tent pins with which he fastened his tabernacle as he pitched his tent toward God. He lived the conquering life because he trusted in God.

This Man Pitched His Tent Toward the Mountains

Thirty-three years ago Edgar Tufts, having just graduated from the Seminary, went out to explore the fastnesses of the yet primeval forest of Western North Carolina. He literally "went out, not knowing whither he went." He went on until he arrived at a little plateau, four thousand feet above sea level, near the headwaters of the Elk, Watauga, Estatoe, and Linville rivers, under the shadows of Beech Mountain on one side and Grandfather on the other. He was a man who had a noble heritage and splendid personal equipment of body, mind, and soul; and he had a driving passion to help the underprivileged and neglected. At Banner Elk, North Carolina, he found the place, the people, and the opportunity he was seeking. From God he received the power to begin to build there an institution with only his dreams as a foundation. A few years ago Edgar Tufts lay down in sleep, secure and happy in the knowledge that a great institution and ideal, visible once only in his dreams, was now taking permanent, unique, and enduring form. His mortal remains sleep just around the corner from the church, built from native stone and beautiful as a work of art. This house of God was the fountain source and effective background for all else he did. He was as surely a hero of the Cross as was David Livingstone. The chairman of the executive committee of the Federal Council of the Churches of Christ in America recently stood by this man's grave and, looking out upon the buildings he had erected, said: "I have been standing to-day on holy ground. I would rather have done the work that my friend and seminary-mate Edgar Tufts has done than that of any man whom I ever knew at the seminary. Having burned out his life in the service of Christ, he died at the comparatively early age of fifty-four." This is a high tribute to a master builder, first of his own life, and next of a great fourfold work for Christ at Banner Elk—an aggressive and strong church, a sterling college with beautiful rock buildings, a Christlike hospital ministering to thousands in nine counties, and a orphanage of the highest type. Being dead, this man yet speaks, not only through his son, who now heads up the work he laid down, but he continues through these institutions, born in his big heart, to proclaim the Gospel, train the minds and bodies, heal the diseases, give the cup of cold water, and in many other ways develop the noble but underprivileged youth in the Southern mountains. Edgar Tufts was immensely wealthy during life and at death. His wealth consisted not in the abundance of things he accumulated, but in great visions of what could be done with his own life, and in and through the lives of the people with whom he labored and wrought. He counted the cost. In this "land of the sky" he charted a bit of God's uncharted world and pushed back the spiritual frontiers. "For which of you wants to build a tower and does not first sit down to calculate the expense? . . . or what king sets out to fight against another king without first setting down to deliberate?" And what Christian, seeking to live the abundant life, the conquering life, sits not down and counts the cost and envisions the results?

WHAT, THEN, IS THE CONQUERING LIFE?

First of all, the conquering life is the Stewardship Life, one that places no value upon anything one has or hopes to possess except in relation to the Kingdom of God, as was the case with David Livingstone. The Steward-ship Life acknowledges God's ownership by reason of creation, preservation, purchase, and sustentation. The Stewardship Life is the conquering life because it is lived in conscious partnership with Jesus Christ. Because this partnership is a covenant with the infinite God, it purifies the heart, clarifies the motives, and energizes the spiritual life. It is partnership in the going enterprise of winning the world to Christ, and one in which the infinite resources of the everlasting God are added to those of the individual.

Jesus said, "I am come that ye might have life, and have it more abundantly." The Stewardship Life is the abundant life. Dr. John Baillie, of the University of Toronto, in his book, "The Place of Jesus Christ in Modern Christianity," warns us against assuming that because we know more than our forbears about science, or about harnessing the forces of nature, that we therefore have a keener knowledge and insight into the ultimate purpose of life. He shows that such questions as, "What must I do to be saved?" and "What is the purpose of life?" cannot be answered out of the head. They demand the answer of the heart. They ask for an answer in the love that suffers and, if need be, dies, as-sured that along such a path of love lies the way to the abundant life. Recently there has come into the book field a number of interesting and helpful books to help us live the stewardship life. Among them are "The Stewardship Life," by Crawford; "Stewardship for All of

Life," by Lovejoy; "Royal Partnership," by Melvin; "The Stewardship of Life," by Agar; "Life as a Stewardship," by Morrill; "Stewardship in the Life of Women," by Wallace, and many others of attractive titles and content. It is significant that all of these find the stewardship life pointing to, functioning in, and guided by the stewardship life as lived by Jesus. In translating Acts 3:15 Moffatt presents Jesus as the "Pioneer" of life. He broke the trail, and He points the way toward complete conquest. Something really worth talking about took place before this "pioneer" made sure the trail that we are to travel to Christian happiness. Something worth talking about took place before it was possible for us to accept Him as the unerring guide and the undeniable example of the simple approach to everlasting power in life conquest.

THE UNHAMPERED LIFE

Second, the conquering life is the life that is freed of its hampering restrictions. I take it that the parable of the king going out to war with the odds two to one against him, teaches us that we can achieve the victory in the battles of life if we will first make the plan of the battle sure. In Revelation 6:2 we have a reference to one "who went forth conquering and to conquer," so that there again is the leadership or there is the "pioneer." In the twelfth chapter of Hebrews we have the conquest likened to a race and the runner is admonished to "strip off every handicap," to "strip off sin with its clinging folds, to run our appointed course steadily, our eyes fixed upon Jesus as the pioneer and perfection of our faith." How often, when we would live the conquering life of happiness and contentment and usefulness, do we find ourselves hindered by sins that beset us, or wills that are weak, or bodies that lack the necessary physical strength to hold out, or minds that are poorly developed, or wills that are insufficiently disciplined. Let us notice some of the things that hamper us and that must be conquered if we are to build a successful "tower" of this life of ours or wage a successful "warfare."

There is the handicap of indolence that must be overcome. Other, and politer, names for it are inertia neutrality, diffidence, and indifference. Worse, but truer, names for it are laziness, procrastination, and sloth. It has been said that four classes of people make up the membership of the Christian Church—the dreamers, the drudges, the drones, and the doers. The dreamers we must have if we would have the doers, but surely there is no room in the conquering Church or in the conquering life for the drudge and the drone! We can accomplish the conquest of Indolence only when we become workers together with God. "We must work the works of Him that sent us while it is day, for the night cometh when no man can work." This means that life—all life—must be built on God's plan, lived in partnership with Him, owing obedience to Him, and built on the high lines of loyalty to Christ. Such a life frees from weakness through physical strength; from laziness through mental alertness; from immorality through moral integrity; from economic dependence through financial independence; and from personal isolation through community responsibility and in doing good to one's fellow men. Laziness can be conquered if we will consider each day's work, whether it be in field or forest, desk or loom, roaring market place or quiet room, as a new opportunity to contribute something anew to the ongoing cause of Christ. From the dark room of my dreams and visions during the night I project a new day's work, and what fun it is to build into the plans for the day, moment by moment, hour by hour, the plans of my invisible but powerful partner, so that at the close of the day I can rejoice and be glad in a work well done.

Another giant we must conquer if we would lead the unhampered life is selfishness. Perhaps the selfish man needs most to orient himself—like the woodsman who climbs the tree to get his directions; or like the ship's captain reading the compass, or taking soundings; like the engineer inspecting his ship. The selfish soul is the soul that is clogged with the "things" of life. The only sure orientation, the only sure cure for selfishness, is worship. Worship means "worth-ship" or "shipworthy." It means that the soul lost through selfishness in the maze of this complex life, and battered by contrary winds, is made shipworthy again because it has found its directions. Worship frees the soul of clogging impurities, delivers it from "repressions," and releases pent-up power. Worship demands solitude, both interior and exterior solitude, and compels the selfish man to face himself—the hardest task he ever does. Worship liberates the personality by giving a new perspective of life, by integrating life with the multitude of life-forces, by bringing into the life the virtues of humility, loyalty, devotion, and rightness of attitude, thus refreshing and reviving the spirit. Worship brings the selfish man face to face with Jesus, and, if engaged in each day, makes of each day a real judgment day. It offers to the man the greatest power in the world—the power of prayer. It opens the door to one who stands there knocking, and, by letting Him in, makes him a partner, and makes available his help in the conquest of selfishness on the road to happiness by way of the unhampered life. "What man . . . sitteth not down first to calculate the cost"—if he would live the conquering life?

The unhampered life is one that accomplishes the conquest of the carnal, by bringing peace to the warfare of the flesh against the spirit—peace through the power and purity of great love. Durant in his "Mansions of Philosophy," a good book on all kinds of etiquette, finds nothing so strange in all history as man's continual pursuit of woman, unless it be woman's willingness to be pursued. He pictures love as the acquisitive advance of the male and the seductive retreat by the female; and yet this fascinating writer finds that over against wealth and wisdom and other things of life, love warms the heart with unspeakable solace, even more when it is given than when it is received.

It is not in life's chances, but in its choices, that happiness comes into the heart of the individual. In making the right choices of friendships and being willing to give as well as to take the love of our friends of the opposite sex, we have one way to conquer the carnal. Dr. William DeWitt Hyde in one of his books on philosophy asks this question: "Do you include the sanctity of the home, the peace and purity of family life, the dignity and welfare of every man and woman, the honest birthright of every child as a part of the social end at which you aim? If you do, you are a noble and honorable man. If you do not, you are a disgrace to the mother that bore you and the home that reared you."

Love that is a conquering love respects personality. The chief sin in pampering, or petting, or fondling, or handling, is just there—an unwillingness to respect the personality of the other person, and by treating the other person as impersonal, as a means to gratify a carnal desire. But love that is true never wantonly wounds nature's crowning achievement—a woman's heart. It is well to remember that monogamy begins long before marriage and lasts all through marriage. But marriage is live's supreme undertaking and test. The glory of modern life, in spite of glaring headlines in the newspapers to the contrary, is the contentment and happiness, the give and take, the acceptance of mutual responsibility and the complete success of the marriage of hearts and lives in the majority of American homes. Although Claudio was mistaken about his assumption of the falsity of Hero, as the story is told in Shakespeare's "Much Ado About

Nothing," he pictured the sad end of falsity in human relations and what happens in may hearts when he said of Hero:

> "But fare thee well, most foul, most fair,
>   Fare thee well, pure impiety and impious purity,
>   For thee I'll lock up all the gates of love."

THE LIFE THAT FACES GODWARD

Third, the conquering life is the life that faces Godward. Our greatest fears arise from our constantly looking at things horizontally. When we look around us it is mostly "things" that we see, and human beings rushing to and fro in search of material possessions, loaded down with the luggage of life. The result of this constantly emphasized perspective is that we too, with a distorted view of their relative importance, begin to seek conquest of life by the accumulation of things. We overdevelop the acquisitive side of life, and leave the spiritual nature underdeveloped. There is only one sure way to cure this desire for things, this overemphasis on the machinery of the present life, and that is, by looking up instead of around; by looking up instead of down; by having first of all the fear of God and thus conquering all other fears.

> "Said the robin to the sparrow,
>   'I should really like to know
>   Why these anxious human beings
>   Rush about and worry so.'
>   Said the sparrow to the robin,
>   'I think that it must be
>   That they have no heavenly father,
>   Such as cares for you and me.'"

210

THE CONQUERING LIFE

The most significant thing, constantly kept before us in the Gospel story, is the way Jesus was always talking to his Father—always looking up for guidance and strength, and always about his Father's business. There is a duty we owe to our fellow men, a duty we owe to our country, a duty we owe to our business interests, and a duty to provide for those dependent upon us. But Jesus would tell us to behold the sparrows, the lilies, the works of God's hand in nature around us. Just as they find, without needing to worry about it, God's provision in things of nature, in the sun, and showers, and seeds, and soil, so may we take a lesson from them by looking up to God for help. It will free our souls from cares that oppress, free our bodies and minds from the luggage of life, and free our hearts of care and burdens.

THE CONQUERING LIFE IS THE CONQUERED LIFE

Fourth, the conquering life is the conquered life. *"Vincer veris"*—I am conquered by truth—is a Latin motto, coming down to us, that expresses the story of a life that, before attempting the conquest of other things or other people, before building the tower of life, or waging the warfare against the forces of the enemy, first goes about the conquest of self. Constantine's slogan for his soldiers was *"In hoc signo vinces"*—"by this sign we conquer." This is the route of conquest over life, by way of the Cross and the Crown of the Saviour. In his book, "The Christ of Every Road," Stanley Jones insists that our lives are never ours until we give them up.

He rightly insists that we cannot go further in the conquest of the individual or the world until we go deeper. He shows that whereas most men live in the three dimensions of prosperity, pleasure, and progeny, the Christian adds a fourth—pain. The Christian who has given over his life in humble submission to him who came that we might have life, and have it more abundantly, has found the route of conquest over all four of the dimensions of life—prosperity, progeny, pain, and pleasure—not of his own strength, but through the strength of another. Dr. John M. Versteeg has written interestingly of Pentecost in a book called "Perpetuating Pentecost." He tells us that the story of Pentecost as recorded in the Bible is not the story of what men did, but of what the Spirit did. Dr. Versteeg is certainly correct. We are reminded of Marshal Foch's statement to the young people of America, when upon being pressed for a message to youth he wrote hurriedly on a piece of paper as he rode down the Valley of Virginia: "I fear God; I have no other fear." Before he conquered the enemy on the Western front he had first of all counted the cost and accomplished the conquest of himself. Therein lies the greatest victory any man can win.

When Robert Tyre Jones, Jr., undisputedly the greatest golfer in the world and the greatest golfer of all time, came back to Atlanta, Georgia, his home town, after having won the British Open, the British Amateur, and the American Open, and having, as a member of the Walker Cup team, helped to win that cup for America, at least one hundred thousand of his fellow-citizens lined the streets to welcome him home as hero and friend. Later "Bobby" Jones accomplished the conquest of the "Impregnable quadrilateral" by winning the American Amateur title, thus becoming the crowned king of the golf world by winning four major titles in one year. At his home club in Atlanta at one time were five cups on display—the Walker, the British Open and Amateur, and the American Open and Amateur. But let us notice the most significant conquest of this young man in the year 1930. It is recorded in an editorial in the *Atlanta Journal,* upon the occasion of Jones's return to Atlanta after the first three of the conquests. After recounting the pride of his home city and home people in his almost superhuman conquest, this paper said: "Our master of golf has first mastered himself; therein lies his topmost trophy."

THE CONQUERING LIFE IS A GROWING LIFE

Fifth, the conquering life must grow. An inventory of life reveals the great tragedy of neglected development. The life is hampered in its joys, the social order lacks the saving salt of contributed ideals, and the Kingdom halts in its march of world conquest because God's people are neglecting a full-rounded development of the forces of life. Growth is not limited by age, except in its physical aspects—and even there, there is room for much improvement of strength and efficiency. Nothing is so much admired as growth in the natural world. We admire the growing tree, the growing plants in the field or garden, and the growing animal life around us. Nothing is so tragic as stunted growth in man who is made in the likeness of God, capable of unlimited growth upward toward God, outward toward his fellow men, and inward toward the things of his soul. How often we find a man who never has known the joys of boyhood—old from childhood—whose schoolroom work was confined largely to the memory, and whose days are indeed as a tale that is told. In the pulpit we find men who were old when they left the halls of the seminary, unchanging in their methods of meeting a changing world's needs. In business, art, commerce, and industry we have the counterpart of this man in the leader who holds back the development of his enterprise because he is bound to the traditions of the past, hampered by a mind that is narrow, or held in check by a soul that seeks to save itself; forgetting that in business, as in religion, "he that loseth his life" in a noble abandonment to a worth-while cause, "the same shall save it."

In the path made plain by Abraham, Isaac, Jacob, Paul, and Livingstone, Samuel Norvell Lapsley of Alabama followed up the Kassai and Luebo to the headwaters of the Congo in Africa. He, too, "went out not knowing whither he went," but brave enough to hear a God-given call to lose his life in a noble endeavor. A graduate of the University of Alabama and McCormick Seminary, he went out with a young negro minister, William H. Sheppard, in 1890. Less than two years later, at Underhill, Africa, a party of new-made friends in a strange land were lowering Lapsley's body in a new-made grave. Less than two years in Africa, but think what he crowded into those two years! Establishment of commercial contacts in London, an interview with the King of Belgium, a perilous voyage to the coast of Africa, a 230-mile tramp by foot from Leopold to Stanley Pool and on by boat and foot to the upper reaches of the Congo, the founding of a Christian mission in an unexplored country; pioneering, living among the cannibals, making his living by his wits, but always conquering in His name whom he served! These are some of the accomplishments of this young man who gave up his life at twenty-six years of age. The natives, unwittingly prophetic, called him the "pathfinder." And so he was. In the establishment of a mission, in his exploration, in his personal growth, he was a real pathfinder. Nothing is so refreshing as the humility of Lapsley. Away in darkest Africa he wrote home to his mother: "I think often of two trips: one to you in the homeland, and another to a lasting Home which I hope to reach after a good deal of the work that I was sent here for. However much time for service He may lend me, it will not be long." Later he wrote: "The thing that I am most ashamed of as I review the six months at Luebo is the small spiritual progress made, and the amount of unimproved time allowed to slip by. I only hope that He who is able is enabling me to improve in both of late." Thus writes and thus lived a great steward of a growing life. When the news of his death was announced by the Secretary of Foreign Missions of the Church that he represented, people everywhere were moved to tears. The glory of that Church lies not, however, in the weeping over his death, but in that she built on the work of this twenty-six-year-old pioneer a great and enduring work in the Dark Continent. As a conquering steward he gave the full measure of a growing life in devotion to the cause of Christ, and, so losing his life, he found life immortal.

The Giant in the Baby Buggy

In the year 1929 there died at Louisville, Kentucky, a man who for fifty-seven years had never walked a step, yet a man who during his life astonished the world in an age of astounding accomplishments. Although a normal child at birth, at one year of age muscular stagnation set in and at fourteen years of age curvature of the spine developed. Considering his growth of body and mind as practically impossible, he was taken out of school at seven. Thereafter all the education that he received was by dint of his own efforts. At his death he was an acknowledged authority on law, an internationally recognized inventor, a painter, an architect, owner of a large manufacturing plant which he operated, an authority on the history of languages, on the great figures of history, on the constitution of the United States, and on art; and withal a lover of all fine things. This man was C. Lee Cook. One of his friends has said: "It is difficult to do justice to this delightful Christian man. It was a pitiful sight to see him pushed along in what looked like an extra well-made baby carriage; but when you looked into his clear, happy face, talked with this man of force, and saw his gentleness, you forgot all notions of pity." This is the man who toiled for twelve years in his father's stable, during his youth, working seventeen hours a day at a lathe of his own construction, turning out a product that earned him a meager five dollars a week, but which laid for him the foundation of his success and brought him happiness, fortune, fame, and a position in the front rank of America's mechanical wizards. At twelve years of age he made a toy boat that would run with steam and pull barges made of cigar boxes. Later he made a steam fire-engine that would throw a stream of water fifty feet in the air, though the engine was only eight inches high. His tools were two files, a hammer, a saw, and a watch-maker's die. One day, while watching the excavation of a railroad cut, he remarked on the excessive loss of steam. He was told that there was no way to prevent it. He set to work on the problem and eventually perfected a steam-packing device, first used on the Louisville and Nashville Railway engines with great economy of mechanical energy. The first one installed ran 175,000 miles without repair. His metallic packing was used during the World War by the emergency fleet, and his lathes by France for making shells. So perfect were his machines that the French informed him that they had not a complaint to make. It was in his twenty-fourth year that a humiliating experience caused him to apply his tremendous energies in broader fields. He was invited to give an address on steel, and did so in a paper that contained amazing prophecies. But his audience tittered. Upon inquiring the cause, he was told by a friend that it was occasioned by the bad grammar and poor composition of his paper. Resolving never again to be guilty of that, he began the intensive study of the grammar, rhetoric, and history of the English language, etymology, and parts of speech. His labors included the compilation of distinctions between 15,000 synonyms and antonyms. He built up a knowledge of roots, original meanings and derivatives, tracing words in Greek, Latin, Hebrew, and Sanskrit. In an examination a few years ago he displayed a vocabulary of more than 37,000 words, a feat believed to be beyond the power of all but perhaps five or six living Americans. It is said that he could transcribe from memory the careers of five hundred of the most famous characters of all time and the conditions under which the people lived during the time of each of these leaders. C. Lee Cook was a man who never ceased to grow by reason of a disciplined will, a trained mind, a channelized intellect. How such a man should inspire old and young alike to an ever-growing life, which is the conquering life!

STEWARDSHIP OF THE FINE ART OF LIVING

At the age of eighty-six years Charles P. Taft of Cincinnati went to his well-earned reward recently. He was a man who never ceased to grow, a man acclaimed on every hand as one of the most admirable and lovable figures in the long period through which he lived a rich and noble life. He was a lawyer, journalist, man of letters, public servant, patron of the arts, and citizen of the wide world. He was loyal to his home city, but equally at home on the Thames, Seine, Rhine, Tiber, or Ohio rivers. With the goodly heritage that was his by birth, with degrees from Yale and Columbia and a background of world contacts, he ennobled his life by growing friendships and made his life a constant benediction to the city of his birth. Among his accomplishments are the drafting of the State of Ohio's first comprehensive and workable plan of education while a member of the legislature; member of the United States Congress; founder of Cincinnati's zoölogical gardens and owner and manager for fifty years of the Cincinnati *Times-Star*. His benefactions to the city include the presentation, jointly with his wife, of the priceless collection of masterpieces in the Cincinnati Institute of Fine Arts and the gift of a million dollars to endow it; the presentation of Barnard's statue of Lincoln to Manchester, England, in the interest of friendship between the nations, and numberless smaller benefactions to his own city. He was friend of his fellow men and friend of God. The munificent gift by Mrs. Taft, following his death, of a giant endowment fund for the study of the humanities, will help to perpetuate his lifelong interest in his fellow men. If we are disposed to class all rich men as sordid, money-grabbers, and material-minded, let us turn aside to look at Charles P. Taft or his noble brother William Howard Taft, for they both illustrate the new type of American mind. They both spanned, in their lives, the era in which we have seen the last frontier wiped out in the West only to be replaced by a new frontier—the main streets of the towns and cities of America, a spiritual frontier where the slogan is supposed to be "that they should get who have the power and they shall keep who can." But the Taft brothers, though rich in this world's goods, never suffered from the overdevelopment of the acquisitive desire to have and to hold property. Theirs was the larger life of happiness in their relation to their fellow men brought about through learning the fine art of living. Until a man has resources within, upon which he may draw with confidence, until he is living a rich life, he can hardly enjoy for his own use, or give away for the use of others, with any degree of satisfaction. Charles P. Taft lived a rich life, for the abundance of the things he possessed were not allowed to interfere with the abundant life of the soul.

Five Great Philosophies of Life

Some thirty years ago William DeWitt Hyde, then of Bowdoin College, wrote a book that has had a great influence on this generation, and has been of great help to the man or woman who, in the quest for safe conduct through life and conquest over the foes of life, seeks for signposts along the way. Dr. Hyde's book, "The Five Great Philosophies of Life," presents to use the five philosophical explanations of life that were current in the five centuries beginning with the birth of Socrates and ending with the death of Jesus. They are: the Epicurean pursuit of pleasure which is, then as now, exceedingly attractive, but stops short of complete satisfaction; the Stoic law of self-control which gives the kind of discipline that is needed in every life, but is personally forbidding; the Platonic principle of subordination of the lower to higher interests, which, though alluring in the sublimity of its ideals, yet is discarded as too ascetic in its interpretation of life; the Aristotelian sense of proportion, of the Golden mean, which appeals to us in its practical aspects, but fails to really inspire; and last, the Christian philosophy, which is love-fulfilling.

It is significant that the great successes of life are those that have been either guided by or inspired by this last philosophy of life. It is not necessary to study the book of Ecclesiastes to know the fruitlessness of the search for safe conduct in the first four of these philosophies, but that book will help the honest inquirer. The writer ends up with the conviction that, after looking for the safe route to personal happiness and testing out the Epicurean life of absorption in pleasure and after trying wisdom and position, and wealth and all others known to the human mind, "all is vanity." "Fear God and keep his commandments; for this is the whole man," is his admonition. This life, which follows the Christian law of love, is a life of continual contribution to God and others. It is the unhampered life, the life that faces Godward, the conquered life, and the growing life.

In "Stewardship in the Life of Youth," by Williamson

and Wallace, a chapter is devoted to the fact that stewardship demands development. The authors say: "He will
hold us responsible for developing into that of which we
are capable, for being that which we have in us to become." Which means that the conquering life is one that
brings to an active partnership with Jesus the best of a
clean body, the keenest powers of a trained mind, the
product of a disciplined intellect and will, and the beauty
of a soul in harmony with the infinite will of God.
Madeline Bridges has finely put it:

> "There are loyal hearts, there are spirits brave,
>   There are souls that are pure and true;
> Then give to the world the best that you have,
>   And the best will come back to you.
>
> For life is the mirror of king and slave,
>   It is just what you are and do,
> Then give to the world the best that you have,
>   And the best will come back to you."

If we were to draw up a creed for practical stewardship living, all of us would disagree on the wording perhaps, but fundamentally such a creed would contain the
following essential items:

A CREED FOR THE CONQUERING LIFE

1. I will subordinate the satisfaction of appetite in order
to live a life of high achievement in the spiritual realm,
considering my term of years on earth more as a training table for the game of life. I will not break training.

2. I will constantly draw upon the resources of my Partner in order to get the reserve strength I need to conquer in times of discouragement, when the odds are against me and fear besets me. I will not quit in the middle of the game.

3. I will live a life of contribution to the general welfare of my fellow men and the upbuilding of the Kingdom of God. When the temptation assails me to put self first, I will subordinate my personal ambition to the interest of the Church, the body of Christ as a whole. I will play with the team.

4. I will control my temper in emergencies in order to give to the task I have chosen as my life work the best of my powers at their maximum calm, realizing that the control of the tongue follows the control of the temper. I will keep my head.

5. I will remember that victory sometimes brings defeat if, in winning, I have sacrificed aught of self-respect, honor, or integrity. Such conquests as I am able to accomplish are the product of others as well as myself. I will be modest in victory.

6. I will win victory in my defeats; for beholding my weaknesses, I will cast myself on Him, and being conquered by Him, I cannot finally lose in life's warfare. I will turn temporal defeat into spiritual victory.

In this time of mass movements, mass production, and mass psychology, when the urge in industry, commerce, business, education, and even in religion is for bigger and better machines and more numbers and better buildings, it is absolutely essential that we center attention on God's providential care for and interest in particular persons. Unless such care is a fact, then life is indeed a "vapor" and a "tale that is told." If such a fact is true, it constitutes my highest incentive to live up to a creed of personal stewardship, and follow God's individual plan for my individual life. By observing the rules, playing the game in a coöperative way, and following through to the end, I can say, with Paul, "I have fought a good fight, I have finished the course, I have kept the faith." The thrilling testimony of a life of conquest is illustrated in Dr. R. J. Campbell's story of the return of David Livingstone to Glasgow as recounted in his "Life of David Livingstone." The students at Glasgow, thinking to have some fun with the missionary, had brought pea shooters and rattlers, determined to drown his talk with their noise. But when the great Livingstone walked on the platform, bearing in his body the marks of conquests over fever, and wild beasts, and tropical exploration, the students were hushed into a great silence. Soon the missionary was telling them about his work for a "Gentleman whose word was never broken," of his following of the One who promised him, "Lo, I am with you alway, even unto the end of the world." The students forgot their previous plans, forgot all else but the matchless appeal of a stewardship life before them, and the appeal of his words that they might lift up their eyes and hearts toward the conquest of the world for Christ.

THE CONQUERING LIFE

This Man, too, Left a Heritage of Conquest

In Atlanta, Georgia, there is a great monument in the very midst of the city to a great Christian steward. On it is this inscription:

HENRY WOODFIN GRADY

JOURNALIST, ORATOR, PATRIOT
EDITOR OF THE ATLANTA CONSTITUTION
BORN IN ATHENS, GEORGIA, MAY 24, 1850
DIED IN ATLANTA, DECEMBER 23, 1889
GRADUATED AT THE STATE UNIVERSITY IN THE YEAR 1868
HE NEVER HELD OR SOUGHT PUBLIC OFFICE
"WHEN HE DIED HE WAS LITERALLY LOVING
THE NATION INTO PEACE"

Upon hearing of his death, the great Chauncey Depew said: "We forget all differences of opinion and remember only his chivalry, patriotism, and genius." He was called by his contemporaries the greatest man of his generation. It is said that there is scarcely a municipal advantage, a public improvement, an educational institution, or an industrial enterprise in the South that does not owe a debt to Henry W. Grady. James Whitcomb Riley said of him:

> "True-hearted friend of all true friendliness,
> Brother of all true brotherhoods."

Wherein lay the secret of this nation-wide conquest of the hearts of his fellow men? Let him answer it, as he speaks before his Alma Mater, the University of Virginia, at the commencement exercises in June, 1889: "The citizen standing in the doorway of his home—contented on his threshold, his family gathered about his hearthstone, while the evening of a well-spent day closes in scenes and sounds that are dearest—he shall save his republic when drum tap is futile and the barracks are empty." Henry W. Grady was a conquering steward who lost his life in a great passion for peace, but found it again in inner happiness through contribution.

If we would live the conquering life, we must begin where Jesus began, he who "made himself of no reputation" and "humbled himself" and became "obedient unto death, even the death of the cross." He counted the cost. He conquered the enemy. He built a towering life, towering still "o'er the wrecks of time." For which of you, intending to build a life, a home, a Church, a state, a nation, or a Christian world of peace and happiness, . . . sitteth not down first to calculate the cost? Stewardship is the acceptance from God of personal responsibility for all of life and life's affairs.

BIBLIOGRAPHY

ABINGDON BIBLE COMMENTARY, THE. Abingdon-Cokesbury Press.

ANDERSON, R. P.: "Studies in Stewardship." International Society of Christian Endeavor.

ATKINS, G. G.: "Procession of the Gods." Harper & Brothers.

BENNETT, ARNOLD: "How to Live on Twenty-Four Hours." Doubleday & Company.

BUTTRICK, GEORGE A.: "Parables of Jesus." Harper & Brothers.

COOK, C. A.: "Larger Stewardship." Judson Press.

CRAWFORD, J. E.: "Stewardship Life." Abingdon-Cokesbury Press.

DURANT, W. C.: "Mansions of Philosophy." Simon & Schuster.

GALSWORTHY, JOHN: "Forsyte Saga." Charles Scribner's Sons.

HAWTHORNE, NATHANIEL: "Mosses from an Old Manse." Boston. 1877. Houghton Mifflin.

HYDE, WILLIAM DEWITT: "The Five Great Philosophies of Life." Macmillan.

INTERNATIONAL CRITICAL COMMENTARY, THE. Scribner's.

JONES, STANLEY: "The Christ of Every Road." Grosset & Dunlap.

STEWARDSHIP PARABLES OF JESUS

Lewis, Sinclair: "Dodsworth." Harcourt, Brace & Co.

Lovejoy, L. E.: "Stewardship for All of Life." Abingdon-Cokesbury Press.

Wallace, Helen K.: "Stewardship in the Life of Women." Fleming H. Revell Co.

Williamson and Wallace: "Stewardship in the Life of Youth." Fleming H. Revell Co.